# ESSENTIAL

# AMERICAN

# GOVERNMENT

## Christopher D.Newman

**KENDALL/HUNT PUBLISHING COMPANY**
4050 Westmark Drive   Dubuque, Iowa 52002

*For Marjorie*
*Without her neither this book nor I would exist.*

The gentleman with the mustache is George Arthur Llewellyn, from my mother's side of the family. G.A. (as he always signed himself) was a scholar at the turn of last century. He was president of Transylvania College in Louisville for a number of years and then went on to head the Bible Department at Texas Christian University. He died raising funds for the move of TCU from Waco to Fort Worth (its present location) after a fire burned the university down in 1902.

The gentleman in the rocker is Frederick Newman (after he Anglicized the name). My Great-grandfather Newman was the kind of person Pat Buchanan hates—after fleeing the Kaiser's draft to fight the Franco-Prussian War as a crewman on a merchant vessel, he deserted his ship in New York harbor and entered the United States in violation of the early immigration laws and fled inland until he felt safe. Evidently he was considerably frightened because he did not feel safe until he reached Kansas. So on my mother's side I come from a line of scholars with a tend toward teaching in colleges, the Newman side finds its roots in an illegal immigrant draft dodger who jumped ship to gain entry.

Here is also a picture of my great-great-grandmother, Elizabeth Anne Bates Cayce, taken in 1933. "Grandmother Cayce" (as she was known to my mother) was a nurse for the Confederacy during what she persisted in calling *"The War of Northern Aggression."* She also occasionally spied on behalf of *"The Cause."* After she married into the family that would produce Edgar Cayce, she became known as one of the first women in the South to *"bob"* (cut short) her hair. Her daughter, Lilla Belle married G.A. Llewelyn, who changed *his* family name to Llewellyn.

The idea is that this is a government *for* all *from* all walks of life.

# TABLE OF CONTENTS

## NOMINATIONS, ELECTIONS AND VOTING

## DEFENSE AND FOREIGN POLICY

## RIGHTS

## OTHER RIGHTS

## INDEX   115

# PREFACE

"They may have taught it to us, but we didn't learn it."

This book should not have had to be written. It began as a result of a panel that was given at the 1994 Illinois Political Science Association meeting. The panel was entitled "Bridging the Gap Between Secondary Schools and Two Year Colleges" and was an excellent presentation on how professors in community colleges should hold periodic meetings with the teachers of social sciences in the secondary schools in their districts for the purposes of exchanging information and teaching techniques.

Unfortunately, *every one* of us in the audience had quite a different idea in mind when we wandered into the room where the meeting was held. Each of us walked in under the impression that this panel would somehow show us how to remedy the lack of preparation we found in our students as they came into our Introductory National Government classes. Each of us had our own horror story to tell (mine was only the most recent—the week before, after ten weeks of my class and years devoted to the study of United States government and history in Third, Eighth and Eleventh grade, one of my brighter students had exclaimed in wonder, "You mean there are *two* houses in Congress? I had always thought there was just the House of Representatives!")

Multiply that story by a room full of people and one can see the difficulties facing college teachers of basic government courses today. The problem was summed up by another of my students in a rare moment of honesty, when he piped up with the quote at the beginning of this Preface. Accordingly, it was suggested that someone should write a brief text designed to acquaint students with the basics of how the United States government does business. I was tapped to do the honor.

My thanks to Connie Anish, Bob Harmon, Pietro Lorenzini and Polly Nash-Wright for their encouragement during the preparation of this text. My gratitude to Tom Fuelling of Morraine Valley Community College who conceived of this project and did not have time to finish it himself, and to Nancy Cerqua of Elgin Community College and College of DuPage, who found time in a busy schedule to edit the original manuscript. Thanks above all to Marjorie Kiefer Newman, who not only provided support for this book at all times, but also prepared the index.

In writing this text I had in mind a book which would be used in much the same way as the Field Manual on Drill and Ceremonies was used during my Basic Training in the Army: each of us found our own copy on our bunk when we arrived and we were informed by our Drill Sergeant that we would be responsible for all the material therein as of reveille the next morning. The Field Manual was direct and to the point and told us everything we needed to know in a way that was easy to understand and remember. I believe this text is as easy to use, as complete and as memorable.

# INTRODUCTION

I have always had difficulty understanding rules if I did not know the reason for the rule. I know that there are a number of people who can function quite well with just a rule and need nothing more, but I have found that the majority of my students need to know the history behind a rule if they are to understand what it means and what it does. Accordingly, this text is intended to provide the context within which the various parts of our political process operate.

In addition, there are other elements of government and society which must operate in conjunction with any part of government for it to accomplish anything, Nothing exists in a vacuum, and the current environment for any government activity is also discussed in this book.

This book starts from the premise that the rulebook which controls every aspect of government is the law. The way that we know what the law means is either through the Constitution, through statutes passed by Congress, or through court decisions interpreting the two. Since the way to know what a law says is through court decisions and since these decisions will also give the historic background of a rule in government, this book will often make use of court cases to explain both context and meaning of our government.

An additional note: unfamiliar terms will be in bold type the first time they are mentioned and will be defined in the text at that time. I have chosen this method to define terms which may be unfamiliar again for the purpose of showing context. It is easier to understand the meaning or a term if you can see how it is used, rather than in isolation in a glossary.

A final note: the Chapter Exercises at the end of each chapter are designed as short essay questions. I have found that students will remember course material longer if they have to use what they learn rather than simply matching or picking "true" or "false." I have also found that using material helps not only retention, but also understanding in the initial learning process. Many of my students do not fully understand concepts until they actually have to use them. The use helps to place the material in a context and the context, to end where we began, helps the learning process.

# CHAPTER ONE

# *Blueprint*

## Chapter Objectives

As a result of studying this chapter, the student should be able to perform the following activities:

1. Explain the two alternative approaches to interpreting the constitution.
2. Explain the organization of the parts of the constitution.
3. Explain the operation of the separation of powers.

## OVERVIEW

The Constitution tells us itself that it is " . . . the supreme Law of the Land. . . . " As such, the Constitution serves two purposes: it acts as a protection of our most basic rights (which will be considered later) and it provides an outline of the setup and function of the national government. It also includes the function of the individual states in relationship to each other and to the national government.

The Constitution was not intended to answer all questions regarding issues that could be considered after 1787. The Constitution was intended to be a sketch or an outline about how the United States is to go about solving problems rather than what the precise solutions were to be. This was made clear by one of the greatest Chief Justices we have ever had, John Marshall. In the case of *M'Culloch*

1

*v Maryland*, 17 US 316 (1819)[1], Marshall's opinion included the basis for interpreting the Constitution and the application of its principles to problems created by changing conditions rather than relying on the simple meaning of its language without exploring any of its implications. Marshall establishes the principle that a constitution is intended as a fundamental law rather than a kind of statute:

> *The subject is the execution of those great powers on which the welfare of a nation essentially depends. It must have been the intention of those who gave those powers, to insure, as far as human prudence could insure, their beneficial execution. This could not be done by confiding the choice of means to such narrow limits as not to leave it in the power of Congress to adopt any which might be appropriate, and which were conducive to the end. **This provision is made in a constitution intended to endure for ages to come, and consequently, to be adapted to the various crises of human affairs.** To have prescribed the means by which government should, in all future time, execute its powers, would have been to change, entirely, the character of the instrument and give it the properties of a legal code. **It would have been an unwise attempt to provide, by immutable rules, for exigencies which, if foreseen at all, must have been seen dimly, and which can best be provided for as they occur.** (17 US at 415) [emphasis added]*

In addition to not being a listing of precise answers for all problems to be encountered after the Constitutional Convention in Philadelphia, the Constitution is not intended to be either convenient or efficient—its cumbersome nature and requirement for slow, deliberate and considered decision making was intentionally built into the nature of the document. As was noted in the case of *INS v Chadha*, 462 US 919 (1983):

> *. . . the fact that a given law or procedure is efficient, convenient, and useful in facilitating functions of government, standing alone, will not save it if it is contrary to the Constitution. Convenience and efficiency*

---

1. In this text we will be using citations to court decisions according the usual legal forms. Citations to Supreme Court cases will be to the official reporter, the United States Reports. Citations will take the form ——US—(date), with the number before the "US" indicating what volume of the US Reports the decision will be found in and the number after the "US" indicating the page on which the decision begins. The year the decision was made is indicated in the parentheses. Direct quotations will take the form —US **at**—, with the number after the "at" indicating the page where the quotation may be found.

*are not the primary objectives—or the hallmarks—of democratic government. (462 US at 944)*

The first part of the Constitution was written in 1787 in Philadelphia.It was written because the first form of government of the United States, the Articles of Confederation, was deemed a failure. Most of the leaders of early America took part in the writing. The primary source that we have about what went on at the Constitutional Convention is from the *Notes of Debates of the Federal Convention,* by James Madison, which Madison withheld from publication until 1840 after all of the delegates to the convention had died. Since Madison was not specifically given the job of officially taking minutes, these <u>Notes</u> are not as full or as formal as minutes of most public meetings, but they will have to serve because they are the only source that we have.

The part of the Constitution written in 1787 is divided into a Preamble and seven Articles. Everything which has been added since 1787 is an amendment (at this writing there have been twenty-seven amendments added with a few others in various stages reaching toward full amendment status.) Most of the Articles and Amendments are further subdivided into sections and many sections are in turn subdivided into clauses. Some of the amendments are concerned with the "fine tuning" aspects of the blueprint of government where unforeseen weaknesses have appeared (for example, the Twentieth Amendment moved the starting dates for the new Congress and new President back to January of the year after the election because it was felt that waiting until March was giving too much time in power to a **lame duck** (or retiring Congressman or President). Other Amendments give us the most basic of our rights ( e.g. the First Amendment gives us the freedoms of religion, speech and the press).

## THE PREAMBLE

The first section of the Constitution is the Preamble and begins the blueprint of our government. Technically it is both the preamble *and* the enactment clause. A preamble explains why this thing is being created—why are we going to all this trouble and what do we hope to accomplish? The things that the Framers of the Constitution hoped to accomplish are many, varied and noble.

" . . . [I]n order to form a more perfect Union . . . " was the major motivation for the Framers, since the United States under the Articles of Confederation had become thirteen small and weak independent nation-states. The government under the Articles had a legislature that met to discuss issues of common concern, but which had no enforcement power, no person or group of people devoted to making sure that the laws passed by the Continental Congress were followed by anyone, and no courts existed to apply the laws except for the state courts. All in all the Articles of Confederation were somewhat less effective at governing the United States than the United Nations is as a world government. There were other goals, some that were lofty, " . . . establish Justice . . . secure the blessings of liberty . . . ", and some that were extremely practical," . . . to insure domestic tranquility, provide for the common defense . . . ." It could be said that the Framers had decided (and hoped that the rest of the country would agree) that accomplishment of these lofty goals depended on achieving practical aims. Then, having set out the goals they were working toward, the Framers inserted the enactment clause into the first paragraph " . . . do ordain and establish this Constitution of the United States". The enactment clause performs much the same starting function for the Constitution as the opening kickoff in a football game: it gets things under way.

The Framers pinned their hopes on creating a viable national government structure as the best means of achieving both sets of goals.Let's take a brief look over the blueprint of the government itself in this chapter.

# THE THREE BRANCHES

Article I sets up the Congress of the United States in some considerable detail (we will explore those details in the chapter on Congress, as we will look more closely at most of the articles and many of the amendments in later chapters specifically devoted to them). All of the powers of Congress are set out, both the general overall legislative power and the specific kinds of things that Congress may pass laws about. In addition to *what* Congress may pass laws about, *how* Congress must pass laws—how a bill becomes a law—is set out in considerable detail. In order to have the *how* of a bill becoming a law, the *who* of the organization of Congress—two chambers, how the members qualify to get there, even who the leaders of each chamber are and how they are selected—are all set out in Article I.

Article II gives us the concept of an executive: someone in charge of making sure that the laws passed by Congress are followed (or,in the words of Article II, "faithfully executed"). The bulk of Article II is concerned with how a President qualifies for his job. It establishes the Electoral College, sets minimum standards for the President, creates the office of Vice President and provides for succession in the event of the death or resignation of the President. Article II also sets forth the powers of the President, both generally ("The executive power of the United States shall be vested in the President . . . ") and specifically ( e.g."Commander in Chief" and "the power to grant reprieves and pardons").

Article III grants the judicial power to the Supreme Court "and to such inferior courts as Congress" may create. Article III is much less detailed in the outline of the court structure than either of the first two Articles, but it does make the independence of federal judges clear through lifetime appointments and the guarantee that judges' salaries will not be reduced. Some kinds of **original jurisdiction** (ability to conduct trials) are specified as being left for the Supreme Court to perform. Article III also gives the Supreme Court final over-all **appellate jurisdiction** (the ability to decide an appeal whether a lower court made a mistake in its decision in a case). The Supreme Court also has the last word on questions concerning the meaning of the Constitution or laws of the United States.

# SEPARATION OF POWERS

The first three Articles, establishing the outlines of the three branches of government, also clearly establishes the principle of the separation of powers: no one who is a member of any one branch of the government can be a member of either of the other two. For example, Article I, Section 7 provides, " . . . no person holding any office under the United States shall be a member of either House during his continuance in office." This stands in stark contrast to Great Britain, where the Prime Minister holds the office by virtue of the position as leader of the majority party in the House of Commons (the British elected legislature). The idea behind the **separation of powers** (making sure that cooperation of separate branches made up of separate groups of people would be required for things to get done) was that each separate group would have its own set of interests and would keep an eye on the other two groups to make sure that neither was abusing their power. Indeed the refusal to cooperate would act as a brake on the abuse. The ideas behind the separation of powers have been considered in a variety of contexts. The first reason for the fragmentation of the power to act among a number of separate entities was to prevent the possibility of concen-tration of too much power in any one set of hands as a means to limit the potential for abuse of power. As was noted in the case of *United States v Brown*, 381 US 437 (1965):

> *The Constitution divides the National Government into three branches—Legislative, Executive and Judicial. This 'separation of powers' was obviously not instituted with the idea that it would promote governmental efficiency. It was, on the contrary, looked to as*

*a bulwark against tyranny. For if governmental power is fractionalized, if a given policy can be implemented only by a combination of legislative enactment, judicial application, and executive implementation, no man or group of men will be able to impose its unchecked will . . . . The doctrine of separated powers is implemented by a number of constitutional provisions, some of which entrust certain jobs exclusively to certain branches, while others say that a given task is not to be performed by a given branch. (381 US at 442–43)*

In addition to making sure that the threads of power are not gathered into too few hands for the sake of freedom, the requirement that a number of consents must be acquired before action may be taken has a practical side as well—the avoidance of being stampeded into hurried and unwise decisions.

*. . . The primary inducement to conferring the power in question upon the Executive [the veto over legislation] is to enable him to defend himself; the secondary one is to increase the chance in favor of the community against the passing of bad laws, through haste, inadvertence, or design.* The Federalist No. 73 *(Alexander Hamilton)*

# OTHER ARTICLES

Article IV provides for both the relations among the various states on a number of issues and is intended to prevent the problem created by the Articles of Confederation which resulted in essentially thirteen independent little nations. Article IV also provides for the creation of new states and the governance by the national government of a United States territory before it becomes a state.

Article V creates the process whereby the Constitution can be changed. Actually this Article provides for the process of changing the **words** in the **text** of the Constitution. We shall see that the words already in the text may be explained or interpreted so as to find certain additional meanings or applications with the text without disturbing the precise wording, just as Chief Justice John Marshall indicated in the opinion in *M'Culloch v Maryland*. In making provision for changing the text of the Constitution to correct mistakes or to meet changing circumstances, the Framers were admitting that they were only human. One is reminded of one of Gary Trudeau's fictional delegates to the Constitutional Convention asking, "What say ye about ye patentability of ye new life forms?" which serves as an illustration of the concept in a nutshell.

Article VI provides, as noted above, that the Constitution is the highest law in the land, superior over all other kinds of law from all other sources. Article VI also provides for payment in full of all debts created by the national government under the Articles of Confederation (in order to preserve the good credit of the United States) and requires that officials of the United States swear to uphold the Constitution. Article VI exempts them from any religious membership requirement to hold office (this was in reaction to the English requirement of membership in the official Church of England to serve in the government—even to go to college).

Article VII provides for the process which will bring the Constitution into force as a legal document: the ratification by nine states at conventions held specifically for that purpose. It is interesting to note that action by nine would bind all thirteen of the states, but eventually all thirteen of the original states ratified the Constitution. All states entering the United States subsequently are assumed to have known what they were getting into and to have accepted the terms of the Constitution when they applied for admission. The new states are, under Article VI, equal in every way to already existing states.

# AMENDMENTS

A number of the Amendments to the Constitution can be viewed as changes in the blueprint of government—tinkering with the blueprint of how government works. The Eleventh Amendment makes it clear that a state can only be sued through its own court system by individuals and not in the federal courts. The Twelfth Amendment provides for the Electoral College to have separate votes for the President and Vice President in order to prevent the candidate for Vice President sliding into the Presidential office by getting more votes through the single ballot of the old system (which almost happened with Jefferson and his Vice Presidential running mate, Aaron Burr). The Sixteenth Amendment permits the Congress to tax incomes. The Seventeenth Amendment provides for the people of a state to elect United States Senators, rather than state legislatures. The Twentieth Amendment moves the starting date for newly elected Congresses and Presidents back to January following the election. The Twenty-second Amendment provides that no one can serve more than two terms as President. The Twenty-fifth Amendment provides for the appointment of a new Vice President if the office falls vacant, making provision for the Vice President to take over as Acting President in the event of temporary Presidential incapacity. The Twenty-seventh Amendment, proposed in 1789 and ratified in 1992 (no, neither date is a misprint), provides that no increase in Congressional pay can take effect until a new Congress shall take office. As we will see, other Amendments assure the rights of United States citizens; primarily the Bill of Rights, War Amendments, and Voting Amendments.

## Chapter Exercises ❖ Blueprint

Name_____ Section_____

1. Your fourteen year old niece is studying for the Eighth Grade Constitution Test. She asks you to explain the separation of powers. Do so, remembering to include (a) whose powers are being separated; (b) why the powers are separated and (c) how and where the powers are separated.

2. She also asks if there is any difference between Articles of the Constitution and Amendments to the Constitution. Is there? If so, what is it?

# CHAPTER TWO

# *Congress*

***Chapter Objectives***

As a result of studying this chapter, the student should be able to perform the following activities:

1. Fully explain the process of how a bill becomes a law.
2. Discuss the leaders and structure of Congress.
3. Define the Elastic Clause and explain how it operates.
4. List the other powers of each chamber of Congress and explain what each of them means.

## HOW A BILL BECOMES A LAW

Article I of the Constitution gives the **legislative power** of the United States to Congress. The process of legislating (passing laws) is the reason for the existence of Congress. The process of how a bill becomes a law is laid out in considerable detail in Article I, a process which has been supplemented by the rules and practices of Congress itself.

The case of *INS v Chadha* explained the reasons for the requirement of so many steps in the legislative process. That case dealt with a Constitutional challenge to the validity of the **legislative veto**, a device whereby Congress kept the power to override any action of an administrative agency by a simple majority resolution of either chamber acting alone. (The theory behind the legislative veto originally was that Congress had created each agency and given it the power to act through the enabling act that called the agency into being, and if Congress wished to place any strings on that grant of power, it felt that it was well within its rights.) The Supreme Court found the reason for the number of steps involved in how a bill becomes a law:

> We see therefore that the Framers were acutely conscious that the bicameral requirement and the Presentment Clauses [requiring Congress to submit a passed bill to the President for his action before it could become law] would serve essential constitutional functions. The President's participation in the legislative process was to protect the Executive Branch from Congress and to protect the whole people from improvident laws. The division of Congress into two distinctive bodies assures that the legislative power would be exercised only after opportunity for full study and debate in separate settings. The President's unilateral veto power, in turn, was limited by the power of two-thirds of both Houses of Congress to overrule a veto thereby precluding final arbitrary action of one person. . . . It emerges clearly that the prescription for legislative action . . . represents the Framers' decision that the legislative power of the Federal Government be exercised in accord with a single, finely wrought and exhaustively considered procedure. (462 US at 951)

A bill must be introduced in either the House of Representatives or the Senate by a member of that chamber. After being acted on by the relevant standing committee and its appropriate subcommittee, the bill may be reported out to the floor for debate and voting by the general membership. (There are ways of getting a bill out of committee if the committee disapproves of the bill, but they are few and far between). After a bill has passed one chamber, it is sent to the other for action. (Actually, what usually happens is that more or less the same bills are considered at more or less the same time by both the House and the Senate, but let's assume that the chambers are acting in sequence).Aside from the slowing of consideration of legislation to avoid the mistakes which flow from hasty decisions, the requirement that both the House and the Senate act before a bill becomes a law, also grows out of the nature of the two chambers— the House being apportioned on the basis of population and being concerned primarily with the needs of the big states; the Senators being apportioned equally to each state, protecting the desires of all states equally—and the Great Compromise that brought both chambers into existence under the Constitution. as was noted in *Chadha:*

> However familiar, it is useful to recall that apart from their fear that special interests could be favored at the expense of public needs, the Framers were also concerned, although not of one mind, over the apprehensions of the smaller states. Those states feared a commonality

*of interest among the larger states would work to their disadvantage; representatives of the larger states, on the other hand, were skeptical of a legislature that could pass laws favoring a minority of the people . . . .It need hardly be repeated here that the Great Compromise, under which one House was viewed as representing the people and the other the states, allayed the fears of both the large and small states. (462 US at 950)*

Once a bill has passed through both the House and the Senate (and a bill means precisely the same bill—word for word and comma for comma), then the bill is sent from Congress to the President where there are four things that the President can do with the bill, 1) the President can sign the bill, whereupon it becomes a law. 2) The President can let the bill sit on his desk for ten days (not counting Sundays); after the end of the ten days the bill becomes law just as if it had been signed. 3) The President can **veto** the bill, suspending its operation as a law and send the vetoed bill back to Congress together with a message detailing the President's objections —if both the House and the Senate vote to override the President's veto by a 2/3 margin or greater, the bill becomes law. 4) If the Congress sends a bill to the President with fewer than ten days remaining before the end of the legislative session and the President does nothing, the bill dies (because the ten days for a bill to become a law required by Article I have not expired and the President has neither signed the bill into law nor vetoed it which sends it back to Congress. This is the dreaded "pocket veto" which confused you so much in grammar school).

This basic outline of how a bill becomes a law illustrates the concept of separation of powers: two or more separate groups required to work together in order for things to get done. Both the House and the Senate must work together for a bill to pass through Congress. In the normal course of events, both the Congress and the President must work together (or at least the President must not oppose) in order for a bill to become a law (the process of veto override requires separate action by an extraordinary majority of each chamber and such overrides are just that—extraordinary). The unlikelihood of an override of a veto, and the great power that the veto consequently gives to the President in the legislative process, is an indicator of the experience of the Framers and their fears of the future in the structure of the national government. As was pointed out in *United States v Brown:*

*The authors of the Federalist Papers took the position that although under some systems of government (most notably the one from which the United States had just broken), the Executive Department is the branch most likely to forget the bounds of its authority, 'in a represen- tative republic . . . where the legislative power is exercised by an assembly . . . which is sufficiently numerous to feel all the passions which actuate a multitude; yet not so numerous as to be incapable of pursuing the objects of its passions . . . ,' barriers had to be erected to ensure that the legislature would not overstep the bounds of its authority and perform the functions of the other departments. (381 US at 443-44)*

# CONGRESSIONAL STRUCTURE

How a bill becomes a law also illustrates the structure of Congress created by Article I. The House of Representatives sits for two year terms with the entire membership standing for election every even numbered year. Representatives must be residents of their states, citizens of the United States, and at least 25 years old. Currently, there are 435 members of the House with the seats in the House divided out among the states on the basis of the population of each state determined in the census (held every ten years in years ending in "0"). The apportionment of representatives among the states is limited by the Article I requirement that each state, no matter how small, must have at least one representative. Within each state, Congressional districts are drawn by the state legislatures. The total of 435 members of the House of Representatives was established by statute (a law passed by Congress) and the size of the House could be changed again by statute. (Incidentally, people often refer to both the House of Representatives and the Senate as "houses" of Congress—I have found this to be the cause of much confusion and will refer to the "chambers" of Congress).

The Senate has 100 members. Article I establishes the size of the Senate at two Senators for each state. Thus the size of the Senate at any time is the result of a simple calculation, two times the number of states. Senators must be citizens of the United States, residents of the states from which they are elected, and at least thirty years old.

Both the House and the Senate have leadership positions, some of which are established by Article I, others are created by statute. The office of Speaker of the House and President pro tempore of the Senate are both recognized by Article I as being full members of their chambers with all the rights and powers which would go along with that status. Article I also makes the Vice President the President of the Senate (that's why the President pro tempore is "pro tempore"), but as President of the Senate, the Vice President only gets to cast a vote to break a tie. Other officers in either chamber are created (and paid) according to statute: House Majority and Minority Leaders— although the *real* House Majority party leader is the Speaker— Assistant House Majority and Minority Leaders, House Majority and

Minority Whips; Senate Majority and Minority Leaders—just to make things confusing, the Senate Majority Leader *is* the leader of the majority party in the Senate, the President pro tempore is the Senator with the longest continuous service traditionally—Assistant Senate Majority and Minority Leaders and Senate Majority and Minority Whips.

# COMMITTEES

The process of how a bill becomes a law also refers to committees. Strictly speaking, that process refers explicitly to **standing committees** and implicitly to conference committees. Standing committees are committees which are expected to continue throughout the entire duration of a Congress, rather than coming into existence for a limited purpose to solve a particular problem of the moment and going out of existence when that purpose has been accomplished (actually we expect standing committees to continue from Congress to Congress, and the birth of a new standing committee or the death of an old one is usually the occasion of widespread discussion).

# CONGRESSIONAL STANDING COMMITTEES

Senate Committees
  Agriculture, Nutrition and Forestry
  Appropriations
  Armed Services
  Banking, Housing and Urban Affairs
  Budget
  Commerce, Science and Transportation
  Energy and Natural Resources
  Environment and Public Works
  Finance
  Foreign Relations
  Governmental Affairs
  Indian Affairs
  Judiciary
  Labor and Human Resources
  Rules and Administration
  Small Business
  Veterans' Affairs

House Committees
  Agriculture
  Appropriations

Banking and Financial Services
Budget
Commerce
Economic and Educational Opportunities
Government Reform and Oversight
House Oversight
International Relations
Judiciary
National Security
Resources
Rules
Science
Small Business
Standards of Official Conduct (Ethics)
Transportation and Infrastructure
Veterans' Affairs
Ways and Means

(from the *Congressional Yellow Book* .Leadership Directories,
   Inc.:January, 1995 p.vii)

Each standing committee is concerned with a particular topic. It deals with bills written about its particular area of concern. Thus farm bills will come before the Agriculture Committee in a chamber, trade bills before the Commerce Committee, and so forth. Because of the bicameral requirement of the separation of powers, each chamber has its own set of standing committees that deal with the topics which confront government so there is duplication of areas of concern, usually with one House and one Senate committee being concerned with the same sort of thing. Sometimes the names of the committees will be different (e.g. Senate Finance and House Ways and Means) but both committees will be concerned with pretty much the same activity (getting money). Each standing committee will have subcommittees which are also organized topically within the general area of concern of the standing committee.

Membership on each committee is arranged as proportional to the ratio of majority party to minority party membership overall in the chamber. The precise number of members on each committee is determined by the majority party at the beginning of each Congress when its caucus sets the rules which will govern the way that Congress conducts business. Assignments to the available seats on a committee are made on the basis of seniority within the majority and minority party ranks. The most senior members (except chamber leaders, who do not sit on committees) get their first choice and then the choice passes all the way down the list of seniority before the most senior member gets his second choice (somewhat similar to what the NFL does with its draft).

Standing committees have a second function closely related to passing on proposed legislation, that of oversight of executive branch agencies. **Oversight**, as the name implies, calls for the standing committees of each chamber concerned with the subject matter of the agency to use its expertise in observing and evaluating how well the agency does its job. This evaluation can be of great importance to the agency as bills that the agency might want to see pass (or corrective measures that the agency would just as soon vanish entirely) must pass through the oversight committees in each chamber before reaching the floor (if at all) for general debate and voting. The oversight function is intended to act as a further check upon potential abuse of power by the executive branch agencies which are largely independent of control within the executive branch itself.

There are three other types of Congressional committees which exist: joint, select and conference. The names of the first two types are descriptive: **joint committees** are committees which have members from both the House and the Senate and **select committees** have members who are specially chosen to deal with a particular immediate problem rather than the membership being put out "for bid" on a seniority basis. **Conference committees** are joint committees of a particular type. Remember that the bill which is sent on to the President for his action must be *precisely* the same coming out of both the House and the Senate. Usually, there will be considerable difference between a bill which is passed the first time by both the House and the Senate. While generally agreeing, there will be variation in details. A conference committee with members from both chambers will resolve the differences with a compromise version which will be reported back to each chamber and then passed by each before being sent on to the President for action.

## OTHER POWERS

Aside from the central function of passing legislation, both chambers have other things that they do: each may subpoena witnesses and compel testimony, and punish reluctant witnesses with jail for contempt. Each chamber is empowered under Article I to judge the qualifications and elections of its members (a statute prevents a majority party from cheating on an electoral count for political purposes). Each chamber has the power to discipline its members to the extent of expulsion by a 2/3 vote. The House of

Representatives has the power to originate all revenue bills (tradition has expanded this Article I grant of power to have the House originate all money bills, including spending); bring impeachment (indict); and elect the President if no candidate has received a majority of the votes in the Electoral College. Article I gives the Senate the power to "advise and consent" (provide necessary approval) of Presidential appointments (by a simple majority) and treaties (by a 2/3 majority); to sit as a jury to try impeachment; and the power to elect the Vice President in the event that no candidate has received a majority of the votes in the Electoral College. The peculiar nature of the exercise of power by one chamber acting alone was noted in *Chadha*:

> *These carefully defined exceptions from presentment and bicameralism underscore the difference between the legislative functions of Congress and other unilateral but important and binding one-House acts provided for in the Constitution. These exceptions are narrow, explicit, and separately justified . . . (462 US at 956)*

In a footnote to that page, the *Chadha* court noted that extraordinary precautions were taken in the very rare instances of one-chamber action.

> *Although the bicameral check was not provided for in any of these provisions for independent congressional action, precautionary alternative checks are evident. For example, Art.II,[Section] 2 requires that two-thirds of the Senators present concur in the Senate's consent to a treaty rather than the simple majority required for passage of legislation. . . . Similarly, the Framers adopted an alternative protection, in the stead of Presidential veto and bicameralism, by requiring the concurrence of two-thirds of the Senators present for a conviction of impeachment . . . a resolution proposing an amendment to the Constitution need not be presented to the President, [but it] is subject to two alternative protections. First, a constitutional amendment must command the votes of two-thirds of each House. Second, three-fourths of the states must ratify any amendment.(462 US at 956)*

## "NECESSARY AND PROPER"

What sorts of things that will be the subjects for legislation are defined by Article I Section 8 of the Constitution. Section 8 consists of Clauses 1 through 18, with the first seventeen clauses being very specific as to powers that are granted to Congress to legislate about (" . . . to lay and collect taxes . . . borrow money . . . regulate commerce . . . among the several states . . . establish a uniform Rule of Naturalization . . . " and so forth.) These specified powers are called enumerated or express powers because they are listed. In contrast, Clause 18 states with sweeping generality that Congress shall "make all laws necessary and proper for carrying into execution the foregoing [Clauses 1–17] powers and all other powers vested by this Constitution in the Government of the United States . . . ." How this Clause 18 is to be interpreted, how much can be read into the words of the Constitution is still the subject of considerable debate between those, like Chief Justice Marshall, who believe that the Constitution must be interpreted broadly and read so as to adapt a living document to changing circumstances. Opposed to Marshall's position are the strict constructionists, who believe that if changes are to be made in the application of the Constitution, they should be made through the amendment process provided in Article V. Strict constructionists fear that straying from the plain meaning of the words used can open the possibility of a Supreme Court interpreting its own political agenda into the Constitution. They believe that the only way to be sure what the Constitution says is not to change its meaning. The question of the meaning of this "**Elastic Clause**", and the standard for Constitutional construction, was first considered in the case of *M'Culloch v Maryland*. In answering the strict constructionists of his day who asserted that "necessary and proper" meant simply that Congress could pay stenographers to record debates and the like, and that if a subject of a piece of legislation was not listed in Clauses 1 through 17 Congress could not write a bill on that subject without amending the Constitution. Marshall noted that such an exhaustive listing of all possible proper subjects necessary to carry out the responsibilities imposed upon Congress would require not a Constitution but a document of great length:

> *A constitution, to contain an accurate detail of all the subdivisions of which its great powers will admit, and of all the means by which they may be carried into execution, would partake of the prolixity of a legal code and could scarcely be embraced by the human mind. It would probably never be understood by the public. Its nature, therefore, requires, that only its great outlines should be marked, its important objects designated, and the minor ingredients which compose those objects be deduced from the nature of the objects themselves. (17 US at 407)*

Marshall interpreted the lists of subjects in the first seventeen clauses as being mere indicators of the sort of things Congress should deal with generally, leaving to the Congress the choice of means under the Elastic Clause to accomplish the vast purposes set out in the Enumerated Clauses:

> *But we think the sound construction of the constitution must allow to the national legislature that discretion, with respect to the means by which*

*the powers it confers are to be carried into execution, which will enable that body to perform the high duties assigned to it, in the manner most beneficial to the people.* **Let the end be legitimate, let it be within the scope of the constitution, and all means which are adapted to that end, which are not prohibited, but consists with the letter and spirit of the constitution, are constitutional.***(17 US at 421)* *[emphasis added]*

## Chapter Exercises ❖ Congress

Name _____ Section_____

1. Explain how a bill becomes a law. Since your explanation should refer to Congressional Committees, explain what different kinds of committees there are in Congress what they do and how they get members,

2. Explain the relationship of the Elastic Clause to the Enumerated Powers in determining what are proper subjects for Congressional legislation.

# CHAPTER THREE

# *The Executive Branch*

*Chapter Objectives*

As a result of studying this chapter, the student should be able to perform the following activities:

1. Name and explain the official and unofficial duties of the President.
2. Explain the functions of the Vice President and the Cabinet Departments.
3. Explain the necessity for "clear guidelines" in an enabling act.
4. Explain the process of rulemaking and ajudication by administrative agencies.

## PRESIDENTIAL DUTIES

The **executive power** of the United States (the power to make sure that the laws passed by Congress are carried out) is given to the President by Article II of the Constitution. The office and person of the Presidency itself have taken on a number of duties: some derived from Article II itself, some acquired over time.

The official duties of Commander in Chief, Chief Executive, Chief Diplomat and Chief Legislator may all be traced directly to Article II. Article II clearly gives the office of Commander in Chief of military and naval forces to the President. The language gives the President the power to issue orders to people in the armed forces and expect that those orders will be carried out. As we will see later in our discussion of defense and foreign policy, the title of Commander in Chief has been interpreted to give the President the power to engage in military adventures as a result of his military office for the purposes of "protecting American lives and property abroad"—a phrase which has been given rather broad interpretation over time.

The President's duties as Chief Executive have been taken both from the grant of the executive power generally in Article II, but also in the power to appoint (subject to Senate approval) the persons who head departments and agencies in the Executive Branch and the ability to require written reports from the heads of the executive departments, and above all, as a result of the obligation that the President has" . . . to see that the laws are faithfully executed . . . " Thus, Article II makes it clear that the President is the person to whom all of the various executive departments report and who has the ultimate responsibility (and presumably authority) to see that the laws are carried out by the other officials in the Executive Branch.

The President's duties as Chief Diplomat are also the result of scattered portions of Article II. The President is given the power to "make treaties" and "nominate ambassadors" subject to Senatorial approval. He is given the power to "receive ambassadors", which has been interpreted to mean that a refusal by the President to receive a government's ambassador means that the government legally does not exist (realities of the existence of government do not matter in terms of recognition of governments—for decades the United States refused to recognize the existence of the People's Republic of China and the government of 1/5 of the world's population). The cumulative effect of all of these powers relating to the negotiation of deals with foreign governments (by making treaties), deciding who is going to be negotiating for the United States (by appointing ambassadors), and deciding who the United States is going to be negotiating with (through the power to recognize governments, taken from the power to receive ambassadors), adds up to the President being the final decision maker with the last word on what the terms are of deals made with other countries.

The duty of Chief Legislator is the result of the requirement that the President "from time to time" report to Congress on how the country is doing— "the **State of the Union**". As part of these reports (which have become the annual State of the Union messages broadcast in January) the President is directed to recommend bills to Congress thought to be "necessary and expedient." This suggestion of bills to Congress that the President thinks are good ideas has led to the precise language of some extensive and complicated legislation being suggested. The effect is that the bill is written out by the executive branch (personified by the President) and then submitted to Congress for its consideration. Typically, a bill proposed by the President will be officially introduced by one of his supporters in each chamber and then will be changed during the legislative process by the House and the Senate.

This specific grant of the executive power to the single person of the President (rather than the collective bodies of Congress) has resulted in an additional duty for the President which can be derived from Article II: Head of State. Whenever the United States needs a single person to stand in for all 250 million plus of the United States citizens, whether it be congratulating winners of the Super Bowl or Nobel Prizes, or meeting the heads of foreign governments, the President is there to represent all of us in the flesh. These activities are enormously time-consuming and are in addition to the already overwhelming jobs associated with running the government discussed above. In Great Britain, the Queen and the royal family perform the Head of State actions and leave the running of the country to the Prime Minister—as the title of the old book had it *The Queen Reigns, She Does Not Rule*[1]. In the United States the President both reigns *and* rules.

As a result of the operation of history, certain additional roles have come to be associated with what the President does. As time has passed, the President has acquired the additional roles of Chief of Party and World Leader. Washington warned in his Farewell Address of the "baneful effects of faction", stating outright that breaking the government and voters up on the basis of political parties after the fashion of England was a bad idea.[2] The problem was that Washington's Secretary of State, Thomas Jefferson, and his Secretary of the Treasury, Alexander Hamilton, had already started what became the first two political parties on the American political scene. (Jefferson's is still with us, although greatly changed, as the Democrats). Since Jefferson's time, it has generally been expected that the President would be the head of his political party. There have been some exceptions. Woodrow Wilson was isolated and bedridden after a stroke toward the end of his term in office and John Tyler was expelled from his political party[3], but generally a President has been viewed as the leader of his party even when leading it to defeat (as was the case with Gerald Ford in 1976 and Jimmy Carter in 1980). The importance of the Presidency in and for a political party

1. *The Queen Reigns, She Does Not Rule,* by F.W.G. Benemy. London: Harrap Press (1963)

2. *The Oxford History of the American People,* Samuel Eliot Morison. New York:Oxford University Press (1965) p346

3. Morison, pp.459–461

can be seen in the fact that a party is not said to be "in power" unless one of its members is in the White House—even if that party controls both chambers of Congress.

A much more recent role which the President has been given is that of World Leader. Because of the functions of Commander in Chief and Chief Diplomat in particular, but also being partially based in the Chief Legislator, Chief Executive and Head of State operations, the President of the United States is a World Leader. Indeed as the leader of the only remaining superpower, the President could probably be viewed as *the* world leader.

# THE VICE PRESIDENT AND CABINET DEPARTMENTS

The Executive Branch is not limited to the President although we usually speak as if it were. The Vice President is also created specifically by Article II. Article II sets out the primary function of a Vice President:spare tire. The Vice President succeeds to the Presidency in the event the President is unable to continue in office. Article II spends a great deal of space discussing how to select a President and Vice President through establishing the **Electoral College** which *actually* elects the President (the votes we cast in November are actually for electors pledged to one or another of the candidates who will then meet to do the actual election of the President and Vice President). Because of the fact that the Vice President may succeed to the Presidency, he is subject to the same qualifications imposed by Article II as the President:over thirty five years of age and a natural born citizen. As noted previously, Article I gives the Vice President the job of President of the Senate, with a tie-breaking vote, and the Twenty-fifth Amendment makes provision for the Vice President to become temporary Acting President in the event the President is incapacitated. Additionally, the statute creating the National Security Council(50 USCA Section 402(a))[4], specifically makes the Vice President a member of the NSC so that

---

4.   Just as we cite to the official US Reports for Supreme Court cases in this text, so we will also cite to the United States Code when talking about official United States statutes. Citations to the United States Code (actually the United States Code *Annotated,* which contains digests of all United States court decisions about each section of the U.S.Code) take the form —USCA Section—. The number before "USCA" is the title of the U.S.Code that the quoted provision may be found in. Title numbers for the U.S.Code are indicated on the spine and cover of each volume of the USCA. The number following "Section" is the section number within the title.

he may be kept aware of the nation's secrets in the event that he must suddenly succeed to the Presidency. The National Security Council keeps track of the United States secret projects and monitors the most secret intelligence reports.

Below the President are the various Executive Departments, each established by statute.(5 USCA Section 101). The Departments are organized topically based upon what they do (e.g. Department of Defense, Department of Agriculture). As previously noted, the executive branch departments, and the agencies that are organized under the heading of each department are evaluated by at least two standing committees of Congress (one from the House and one from the Senate) which perform the function of legislative oversight for the departments and agencies working on the same kinds of topics as the standing committees deal with in legislation. The heads of each Department (together with some other people that a particular President may give "Cabinet Rank" to) make up the President's Cabinet and are expected to advise the President in decision making and to run their respective departments.

# THE DEPARTMENT OF THE EXECUTIVE BRANCH

Department of State

Department of the Treasury

Department of Defense

Department of Justice

Department of the Interior

Department of Agriculture

Department of Commerce

Department of Labor

Department of Health and Human Services

Department of Housing and Urban Development

Department of Transportation

Department of Energy

Department of Education

Department of Veterans Affairs

(from 5 USCA Section 101)

# ADMINISTRATIVE AGENCIES

If one were to look at a diagram describing the operation of the Executive Branch, it would look like each department had a number of administrative regulatory agencies which were attached to it . These agencies are sometimes called independent agencies because they are supposed to be beyond direct influence for political purposes. They are also called alphabet agencies because they are commonly referred to by their initials (e.g. FCC,SEC,FTC)

These regulatory agencies are the portions of the federal government that we come into contact with on the most frequent basis. It is the EPA that regulates how much exhaust comes out of our cars, the FDA that regulates what goes into our mouths, the IRS that takes a large fraction of our paychecks. In the process of regulation, the administrative agencies take the language of statutes passed by Congress and applies those laws directly to daily life.

This application of federal statutes to daily life by the administrative agencies is accomplished through two main types of processes: rulemaking and adjudication. **Rulemaking** is the process where an agency takes the general language of a statute and explains what it means in a particular context. **Adjudication** is the process used by the agency to determine whether or not someone has violated one of its rules and impose penalties. In rulemaking an agency is acting like Congress when Congress is passing laws, in adjudicating the agency is acting like a court.

This Congresslike and courtlike activity, dressed up in legal Greek as **quasilegislative** ("like legislative") and **quasijudicial** ("like judicial") activity, was the basis for the Supreme Court decisions of *Humphrey's Executor v US*, 295 US 602 (1935) and *Wiener v US*, 357 US 249 (1958). These cases give the administrative agencies independence from Presidential control on the basis of the separation of powers. The Supreme Court reasoned that a President firing someone in an agency engaged in quasilegislative or quasijudicial activity was just like the President attempting to fire someone in the Congress or the federal courts. The independence of Congress and the courts was established by the Constitution. By extension the independence of the administrative agencies engaged in regulation would also be preserved.

This is not to say that the administrative agencies are without limits in their actions: both the rulemaking process and adjudication are governed by the Administrative Procedure Act of 1946. Each agency is also limited by the particular statute that created it. Such statutes which create an agency and give it the power to act are called **enabling** acts because they enable the agency to perform its regulatory activity.

Each enabling act, when it is creating an agency, states what it is that the agency is intended to do. Outer limits are also set within which the agency performs its activities. These limits must be present when the agency is given power to act. The Supreme Court has determined that,if Congress were to turn an agency loose without placing any limits on what the agency could do, Congress would be giving the power to legislate to the agency. This would be unconstitutional as a violation of Article I, Section 1, which gives the legislative power of the United States to Congress and Congress alone.

The courts have also determined that the limits set by Congress do not have to be terribly well defined; indeed, although they are called **"clear guidelines"**, these outer limits set for the operation of each individual are frequently very ambiguous—e.g. the Federal Trade Commission regulates "unfair trade practices." If Congress wishes to change an agency action, the fact that Congress set the "clear guidelines" means that Congress has the power to alter the agency decision by statute. As was noted in *Chadha:*

> *That kind of Executive action is always subject to check by the terms of the legislation that authorized it; and if that authority is exceeded it is open to judicial review as well as the power of Congress to modify or revoke the authority entirely. (462 US at 953)*

In the rulemaking procedure, the process explains in particular concrete fashion what the clear guidelines mean in particular cases. The Administrative Procedure Act sets up the precise steps which an agency must take in order to officially explain what was meant by a particular clear guideline. The steps are fairly simple. A notice of a proposed rule must be published in the *Federal Register* (an official magazine published by the U.S. government every business day designed to give official notices of this sort); a period of time, at least thirty days, must pass during which time parties who are in favor of or opposed to the rule may send their comments to the agency; finally a notice of the final form of the rule must be published in the *Federal Register* which upon publication the rule becomes effective. Rules of an agency are not written in stone. It is always possible to ask or petition the agency to change or repeal the rule if it can be shown that the rule is not working out.

Just as the process for making rules is specified for all administrative agencies in the Administrative Procedure Act, the Act also specifies the process that an agency must go through in order to determine whether or not one of its rules has been violated. The quasijudicial or adjudication process specified in the Administrative

Procedure Act is very similar to a bench trial in a regular court, where the judge sits as both **finder of law** (the traditional judge function) and **finder of fact** (the traditional jury function). In an adjudication process the judge role is played by a hearing officer. In order to make sure that there is no undue influence on the hearing officer by the agency, which is also the plaintiff in these actions, there is a mini-separation of powers within the agency, with the hearing officers separated from the enforcement branch of the agency. Otherwise, the proceeding is similar to a trial. Witnesses with evidence for one side are tested through cross-examination by the other side followed by a reversal of the process with the hearing officer having the opportunity to see the strengths and weaknesses of each side's strongest case and thus being able to decide which side should win. Both the Administrative Procedure Act and the enabling act of each particular agency with greater detail, determine where and how appeals will be taken if a party disagrees with the decision of the hearing officer.

## Chapter Exercises ❖ The Executive Branch

Name _____Section_____

1. Explain the official and unofficial duties of the President to your niece, who is still studying for the Constitution Test.

2. Your uncle wonders about the latest program of the EPA to cut air pollution by forcing car pooling. Explain to him the concepts of (a) clear guidelines in an enabling act; (b) the rulemaking process; and (c) administrative agency adjudication as explaining how an administrative agency might be able to improve air quality.

# CHAPTER FOUR

# *Courts*

### Chapter Objectives

As a result of studying this chapter, the student should be able to perform the following activities:

1. Explain standing and jurisdiction and their importance in beginning a trial.
2. Explain how a trial and subsequent appeals are conducted.
3. Explain the overall structure of the federal court system.
4. Explain the importance of the decision in *Marbury v Madison* to the power currently exercised by the federal courts.
5. Explain the process of finding a United States statute unconstitutional.

## OVERVIEW

The federal court system may be thought of as a pyramid of three levels, one with a broad base of many district courts, a second level of twelve Circuit Courts of Appeal, and a point on top that consists of the Supreme Court of the United States. Each level has its own particular function in the scheme of things. Our pyramid is incomplete. There are a number of specialized courts feeding into the Court of Appeals for the Federal Circuit.

The courts at each level are organized on a geographic basis with each District Court having a slice of territory that it has power over to enforce its will. Each Circuit Court controls the territories of a number of District Courts and the Supreme Court reigns over the entire territory of the United States.

A major difference between the judicial branch and the **political branches** (Congress and the Executive Branch) is the fact that the judiciary is largely the creation of statutes rather than the Constitution. The Supreme Court is specifically provided for in Article III, but after that there are references only to "inferior courts" subsequently to be created by Congress. Article III does provide guarantees of the independence of federal judges (by providing for lifetime appointment "during good behavior" and by assuring that their salaries cannot be reduced) and does provide a specific list of subjects of federal trial jurisdiction, including those few kinds of cases that the Supreme Court hears as a matter of original (trial) jurisdiction, in addition to the more frequent appellate jurisdiction.

# STANDING AND JURISDICTION

On the front line of dispensing federal justice are the District Courts—courts of original jurisdiction or trial courts. In order to have a trial, a court must have a case brought to it for a decision (unlike the political branches, which are active bodies and may go out on their own to find problems to solve, courts are *reactive* bodies which must wait for others to bring problems to them for resolution). The person bringing the case to the court (the person suing) is called the **plaintiff** (even in criminal cases, "The People of—" charging the defendant with a crime act as the plaintiff; to make this easy we will stick to civil suits and private parties, but the parallels exist in criminal actions). The person being sued is called the **defendant**. In order to bring suit, the plaintiff must have **standing**. In order to have standing, two conditions must both be satisfied: 1) the plaintiff must have suffered some harm (e.g. physical or financial); and 2) the defendant must have owed the plaintiff a duty (society must have said to defendant officially that there are some things he must do for the plaintiff and some other things the defendant must not do to the plaintiff) which was violated. If the plaintiff has satisfied both conditions, then he has standing and can proceed to the courthouse.

The question of *which* courthouse is tied up in quandaries concerning jurisdiction. **Jurisdiction** answers the question,"Is this the kind of case this court hears?", but this is a question with shifting emphasis. The first way to ask the question is to emphasize the question of the particular court, "Is this the kind of case *this court hears?*" In other words, is the defendant within the slice of territory that this particular court controls Although first asked at the District Court level, the same question is asked to determine which Circuit Court of Appeal the case will go to if necessary. If the answer is "Yes", then the court has **jurisdiction of the person** over the defendant—it can enforce its orders on him and make them stick.

The emphasis shifts in the question, "Is this *the kind* of case this court hears?" The various subjects that federal courts will consider have been outlined in Article III and then fleshed out by statute. **Jurisdiction of the subject matter** (the kinds of cases federal courts will hear) fall into three broad categories:

1. diversity jurisdiction involves suits between plaintiff and defendant who are citizens of different states (remember that the suit still has to be brought in the Federal District Court where the defendant lives, but the independence of the federal judiciary is supposed to assure a more level playing field for the plaintiff from out of town);

2. federal questions are suits based on the Constitution or federal statutes; and

3. admiralty, concerning any suits about ships "on navigable waters", i.e. where you can drive them.

# ADVERSARY PROCESS

At a trial there are both parties, their lawyers, a judge and a "finder of fact" (usually a jury). Witnesses are called by both sides, with their evidence being given for the side that called them and then their story tested by cross-examination. Unfriendly questions from the other side are designed to show weakness in the opponent's case. Along the way the judge will make decisions about **questions of law**, usually whether a question may be asked or a witness allowed to testify. The jury observes the witnesses testify and decides which story to believe, or decides **questions of fact**.

This presentation of each side's strongest case, with the opposition showing the weaknesses in that strongest case observed by an impartial third party acting as a finder of fact, is called the **adversary process**. The nature of the adversary process was discussed in *United States v Nixon*, 418 US 683 (1974):

> *We have elected to employ an adversary system of . . . justice in which the parties contest all issues before a court of law. The need to develop all relevant facts in the adversary system is both fundamental and*

*comprehensive. The ends of . . . justice would be defeated if judgments were to be founded on a partial or speculative presentation of the facts. The very integrity of the judicial system and public confidence in the system depend on full disclosure of all the facts, within the framework of the rules of evidence. (418 US at 709)*

The nature of the adversary process, which necessarily depends on both sides in a trial putting forth their best efforts, gives rise to one of the two self-imposed limits, the **"case or controversy" rule**: courts will not hear a trial (in the words of *Chadha)* which is "a friendly, non-adversary proceeding". A court will only entertain an action in which there is a "concrete controversy" (462 US at 939).

The second self-imposed limit that courts will employ are those of **"political questions"**. A court will not conduct a trial on issues which are more properly dealt with by the political branches. The so-called "one man-one vote" case, *Baker v Carr,* 369 US 186 (1963), is the lead case on political question and related judicial restraint. That decision set forth the nature of and reasoning behind the creation of the rule:

*It is apparent that several formulations which vary slightly according to the settings in which the questions arise may describe a political question, although each has one or more elements which identify it as a function of the separation of powers. Prominent on the surface of any case held to involve a political question is found a textually demonstrable constitutional commitment of the issue to a coordinate political department; or a lack of judicially discoverable and manageable standards for resolving it; or the impossibility of deciding without an initial policy determination of a kind clearly for nonjudicial discretion; . . . or an unusual need for unquestioning adherence to a political decision already made; or the potentiality of embarrassment from multifarious pronouncements by various departments on one question (369 US at 217)*

# CONGRESSIONAL LIMITATION

The "case or controversy" rule and the "political question" rule limiting judicial consideration of a case are self-imposed, a form of self-control. As everyone who has been on a diet knows, self-control does not always prevent taking an action. In contrast, a third limitation on the power of courts to hear cases is imposed from outside by Congress and is mandatory, rather than discretionary, for a court. Congress has the power by statute to remove an entire class of cases from the jurisdiction of the courts. This was most clearly seen in *Ex parte McCardle*, 74 US 506 (1868). In that case McCardle was a newspaper editor in Mississippi who was jailed for publishing "incendiary and libelous articles" by the military authorities operating under the terms of the Reconstruction Acts. McCardle filed for a writ of *habeas corpus* (essentially "charge me with a crime or let me go") under the Constitution. His petition for the writ was rejected and he appealed to the Supreme Court as he was authorized to do under the Judiciary Act of 1867. The Court heard argument and retired to consider its decision. Before the Court held its conference to consider its decision in *McCardle,* Congress specifically repealed that portion of the Judiciary Act of 1867 authorizing appeals of *habeas corpus* petitions to the Supreme Court. As the Court noted in its later *McCardle* opinion, "It is hardly possible to imagine a plainer instance of [withdrawal of jurisdiction]" (74 US at 514). The Supreme Court then considered the effect of the Congressional statute withdrawing jurisdiction:

> . . . *[T]he power to make exceptions to the appellate jurisdiction of this court is given by express words.*

> *What, then, is the effect of the repealing Act upon the   case before us? . . . Without jurisdiction the court cannot proceed at all in any cause. Jurisdiction is the power to declare the law, and when it ceases to exist, the only function remaining to the court is that of announcing the fact and dismissing the cause. (74 US at 514)*

## COURTS OF APPEALS

The loser at the trial level may appeal to the next highest level, in this case to the appropriate Circuit Court of Appeals. Although there are a number of judges with positions on each Circuit Court, (anywhere from six to twenty-six, depending on the Circuit) each appeal will be heard by a panel of only three judges chosen at random. "Heard" is a misnomer. Most appeals have judges reading documents, " briefs," or statements of each side's position, transcripts of the testimony at trial. The three judges will rarely hear what is called oral argument, where both sides are asked questions about their case by the appellate judges. The appellate judges may decide **questions of law** ("Did the trial judge make a mistake in rulings in the conduct of the trial?") but they may not decide **questions of fact** ("Which witness was more believable?") because they did not *see* the testimony and thus were not in as good a position as the jury to use things such as tone of voice and facial expression to fully evaluate the truthfulness of each witness.

# THE SUPREME COURT

Losers at the Circuit Court level may *ask* the Supreme Court to hear their further appeal. The Supreme Court does not have to accept the appeal, and in the overwhelming majority of cases submitted for Supreme Court consideration does not do so. If four or more Justices of the Supreme Court wish to hear the appeal of a case, it will be heard (the **"Rule of Four"**). Again there are briefs presented by each side, again transcripts and evidence are examined, again occasionally oral argument may be presented if the Justices wish to hear it. After all material has been presented, the Justices will retire to consider their decision.

The Supreme Court has three ways in which it will reach a decision on an appeal (actually all appellate courts will follow this overall plan, it's just easier to see the operation of "overrule" at this level as lower courts may not overrule the decisions of higher courts). The first way is by far the most common: " we've already decided a case before which was like this one in all important respects, so we'll decide this case the same way as that prior case" (**stare decisis**, Latin for "the thing is decided"). The second way of deciding an appeal is to look at prior cases and say "We've already decided a case like this before, but that prior decision was a bad result and established a bad principle of law, so we'll kill off that prior case (**overrule** it) and decide the present case in a different way so as to establish a new set of principles of law." Both the first two ways of deciding are based on the idea that a prior case dealt with the subject matter of the present case. The third way of deciding is reserved for those kinds of cases which are new. When a completely new kind of case is to be decided the court says "it's new" (in Latin) or **de novo** and acknowledges that there are no precedents available for direct guidance.

Some courts were created by Congress to deal with very technical and specialized areas of the law (for example, Tax Court or the Court of Claims). These specialized courts, and their own specialized Court of Appeals, the Court of Appeals for the Federal Circuit, deal only with cases arising within their narrow area of expertise (although it should be noted that the Supreme Court may hear appeals from these as well as all the other federal courts.)

The Supreme Court has a number of responsibilities which flow from its position at the top of the judicial pyramid. It stands as the final authority in dispensing justice and determining questions of law with the power to correct all mistakes made by lower federal courts. It stands as the final authority in interpretation of the Constitution and federal statutes with the power to decide absolutely (subject, of course to a decision by a later Supreme Court) what the Constitution and the laws passed by Congress mean.

It stands as the final authority in Judicial Review determining if laws and actions of any government in the United State are void as unconstitutional. These powers of the Supreme Court all grow out of the decision of *Marbury v Madison*, 5 US 137 (1803).

# MARBURY v MADISON

The *Marbury* case grew out of last frantic hours of the John Adams administration, when Adams and the Federalists truly believed that Thomas Jefferson and the Republican-Democrats (who we now call the Democrats) were going to bring the worst parts of the Terror of the French Revolution to the United States with Jefferson's assumption of the Presidency. Adams and the Federalists tried to control the last branch of the Government left to them, the Judiciary, by appointing a number of good Federalists to positions as magistrates and judges. Marbury was one of seven appointed as magistrates for the District of Columbia, their commissions appointing them completed but undelivered by the outgoing Secretary of State. The incoming Secretary of State, James Madison, refused to deliver the certificates of office and prevented anyone from his office from even testifying in any of the formal and informal proceedings Marbury and the others had started to gain their already-completed appointments. What the Federalists were seeking was a particular order, a writ of mandamus, which was an order from the Supreme Court to some officer of the U.S. government to perform a duty that he was obligated to perform. This kind of *must do* action, in which the governmental official is turned into a sort of robot operating to carry out someone else's orders, is called a *ministerial* function. It is contrasted with the more common *discretionary* action, in which the official exercises his best judgment. Marbury and the rest relied upon the Judiciary Act of 1795, which granted the power to the Supreme Court to issue writs of mandamus as parts of its original jurisdiction, or trial court power.

After finding that Marbury and the others had an absolute right to their offices as magistrates:

> *"The discretion of the executive is to be exercised until the appointment has been made. But having once made the appointment, his power over the office is terminated in all cases . . . . The right to the office is then in the person appointed, and he has the absolute right of accepting or rejecting it . . . . To withhold his commission, therefore, is an act not warranted by law, but violative of a vested right. (5 US at 162)*

Marshall read the Judiciary Act and noted that its specific grant of the power to issue writs of mandamus caused confusion when compared to the section of Article III which had a slightly different list of grants of original jurisdiction, with Article III omitting the mandamus power. The question of who was to reconcile the differences between the Constitution and the statute was clear:

> *It is emphatically the province and duty of the judicial   department to say what the law is. Those who apply the rule to particular cases, must of necessity expound and interpret that   rule. If two laws conflict with each other, the courts must decide on the operation of each. ( 5 US at 177)*

Thus the courts, by the very nature of their status as courts, had the power and responsibility to decide what to do in the case of a conflict between a statute passed by Congress and the Constitution. The answer followed from the nature of the Constitution itself:

> *This original and supreme will organizes the government and assigns to different departments their respective powers. It may either stop here, or establish certain limits not to be transcended by those departments.*
>
> *The government of the United States is of the latter description. The powers of the legislature are defined and limited; and that those limits may not be mistaken, or forgotten, the constitution is written.(5 US at 177)*

From the realization that the provisions of the Constitution are superior to any other form of law, statutory or common, the conclusion was inescapable:

> *Certainly all those who have framed written constitutions contemplate them as forming the fundamental and paramount law of the nation, and, consequently, the theory of every such government must be, that an act of the legislature, repugnant to the constitution, is void.(5 US at 177)*

Notice what Marshall has done here. Without any specific grant of authority in Article III, he has (1) grasped the sole power to say what the Constitution means for the courts; and (2) also given the courts the power to declare acts of the other two branches null and void. Thus, the position of the Supreme Court as the final authority in American politics is more the creation of John Marshall than the Framers of the Constitution.

# Chapter Exercises  Courts

Name_____Section_____

1. One of your friends was fraudulently sold a dead parrot while he was out of state. Explain to him all the steps necessary to bring his suit to recover the cost of the bird, and, if necessary, appeal all the way up through the United States Supreme Court. (In order to make this a federal problem, assume that your friend is both naive and rich and paid $100,000 for the dead bird.)

2. What major increase in the power of the federal courts did John Marshall accomplish in *Marbury v Madison*? How did he do it?

# CHAPTER FIVE

# *... and the States*

The topic of federalism may be divided into three basic subdivisions:

1. the nature of relations of the federal government with the state governments;
2. the nature of the relations among the governments of the various states; and
3. the nature of the state governments themselves.

# FEDERAL SUPREMACY

The question of the relationship between Congress and its statutes on the one hand, and the states and any measures that they might employ to frustrate a Congressional statute on the other, was considered initially in *M'Culloch v Maryland* . Aside from providing the basic principles of interpreting the Constitution, the *M'Culloch* case dealt with questions involving measures taken by Maryland to frustrate the operation of the Bank of the United States's within the boundaries of that state. Specifically, Maryland had imposed a prohibitive tax on certain operations of the Bank with an eye to making it economically impossible for the Bank to operate.

In finding the Maryland measures unconstitutional (and giving us the ringing phrase "The power to tax is the power to destroy!"), Chief Justice John Marshall found that actions of a whole must necessarily take precedence over the actions of a part. Conversely the independent will and actions of a part should never operate, or be permitted to threaten to operate, so as to frustrate the actions of its whole:

> *No trace is to be found in the constitution of an intention to create a dependence of the government of the Union on those of the states, for the execution of the great powers assigned to it. Its means are adequate to its ends; and on those means alone was it expected to rely for the accomplishment of its ends. To impose on it the necessity of resorting to means which it cannot control, which another government may furnish or withhold, would render its course precarious; the result of its measures uncertain, and create a dependence on other governments, which might disappoint its most important designs, and is incompatible with the language of the constitution.(17 US at 424)*

Since permitting the Maryland tax to stand would be the same as allowing Maryland to indirectly prohibit the operation of a Congressional statute, just as effectively as a Maryland act directly prohibiting the operation of a Congressional statute, the Maryland tax is found unconstitutional using the same procedure set up by Marshall in *Marbury v Madison:*

> *The result is a conviction that the states have no power by taxation or otherwise to retard, impede, burden, or in any manner control the operations of the constitutional laws enacted by Congress to carry into execution the powers vested in the general government. That is, we think, the unavoidable consequence of that supremacy which the constitution has declared. (17 US at 437)*

The reasoning that led to the result of finding state legislation necessarily subordinate to valid conflicting federal legislation was logically developed from the Article VI Supremacy Clause:

*This great principle is, that the constitution and the laws made in pursuance thereof are supreme; that they control the constitution and laws of the respective states, and cannot be controlled by them. From this, which may be almost termed an axiom, other propositions are deduced as corollaries, on the truth or error of which, and on their application to this cause has been supposed to depend. These are, 1st. that a power to create implies a power to preserve. 2d. That a power to destroy, if wielded by a different hand, is hostile to, and incompatible with these powers to create and preserve. 3d. That where this repugnancy exists, that authority which is supreme must control, not yield to that over which it is supreme. (17 US at 426)*

The principle of state action necessarily yielding to conflicting federal action established the supremacy of the federal government when it was validly exercising its powers. The question of validity in turn was based upon the question whether the exercise was among the enumerated powers specifically granted to the branches of the federal government by Articles I, II or III; or whether such an exercise of power could be fairly implied from the enumerated power which was asserted as the source of the implied power (the Elastic Clause in Article I Section 8, with its "necessary and proper" language is the clearest standard for a basis for interpretation of the existence of such a derivative power).

Recall that Marshall interpreted the very power to authoritatively interpret the Constitution itself, together with the power to find an action of a government unconstitutional, with much less authority to go on. Starting with only the nature of a judiciary as a basis for his decision in *Marbury v Madison,* there was not even an enumerated power as such to serve as a hook to interpret into existence *the power to interpret* **itself**.

Similarly, the power of the President to recognize foreign governments, although derived from the enumerated power of receiving ambassadors, is not derived from that enumerated power according to any constitutional formula along the lines of the "necessary and proper" clause of Article I.

The necessity of finding some basis in the relevant Article of the Constitution to justify the validity of any power asserted by the federal government has tied the federal government to those three Articles in terms of the kinds of things that the federal government can do and the ways in which it can do them.

In regard to the relationship between the federal government and the states, the Tenth Amendment speaks directly to the question of powers not swept up in federal net, "The powers not delegated to the United States by the Constitution, nor prohibited by it to the States, are reserved to the States respectively, or to the people." The distinction between the nature of the exercise of power by the federal government on the one hand and the nature of the exercise of power by the states on the other was noted by the Supreme Court in *Cohens v Virginia*, 19 US 264 (1821):

> ... *[T]he characteristic distinction between the government of the Union and those of the states. The general government, though limited as to its objects, is supreme with respect to those objects. This principle is a part of the constitution [Article VI, the Supremacy Clause]; and if there be any who deny its necessity, none can deny its authority. (19 US at 381)*

The case in *Cohens* dealt with defendants who had been arrested by Virginia authorities for selling federal lottery tickets. The Cohens claimed that they were protected from arrest by the federal statute establishing the lottery, stating that they were the duly authorized agents for the sale of the tickets. The Virginia authorities agreed that the Cohens were protected by federal law, but then Virginia claimed that the state criminal prosecution was not subject to review by the United States Supreme Court, even though a question of the relative supremacy of the state and federal statutes was involved.

The Supreme Court began its determination as to whether it had jurisdiction to review and potentially overrule a state court decision with an historical analysis of the original purpose for creating the Constitution to replace the old Articles of Confederation:

> *The American States, as well as the American people, have believed a close and firm Union to be essential to their liberty and to their happiness. They have been taught by experience, that this Union cannot exist without a government for the whole; and they have been taught by the same experience that this government would be a mere shadow, that must disappoint all their hopes, unless invested with large portions of that sovereignty which belongs to independent states. Under the influence of this opinion, and thus instructed by experience, the American people, in the conventions of their respective states, adopted the present constitution. (19 US at 380)*

The Supreme Court then noted that the jurisdiction of the federal judiciary was derived in part, according to Article III, from cases arising under the laws of the United States. The Cohens asserted the protection of a federal statute. Virginia claimed that the Supreme Court could not determine whether or not the Cohens were correct, i.e. Virginia claimed that the Supreme Court could not interpret the federal statute to determine whether it applied to state court proceedings; that state courts were immune from any judicial authority but their own. The Supreme Court in *Cohens* noted what the result of the Virginia position would be on the scheme of an integrated national whole that motivated the establishment of the Constitution:

*The mischievous consequences of the construction contended for on the part of Virginia are also entitled to great consideration. It would prostrate, it has been said, the government and its laws at the feet of every state in the Union. . . . What power of government could be executed by its own means, in any state disposed to resist its execution by a course of legislation? The laws must be executed by individuals within the several states. If these individuals may be exposed to penalties, and if the courts of the Union cannot correct the judgments by which these penalties may be enforced, the course of government can be, at any time, arrested by the will of one of its members. Each member will possess a veto on the will of the whole. (19 US at 385)*

Thus we are back to the same analysis of the part being subordinate to the will of its whole that we saw in *M'Culloch*. Basing the final holding in *Cohens* on the superiority of the whole to the part, as well as the necessity for a supreme single government as a necessity for a single integrated nation, Chief Justice Marshall summed up his position on the supremacy of the national government:

*That the United States form, for many, and for most important purposes, a single nation, has not yet been denied. In war, we are one people. In making peace, we are one people. In all commercial regulations, we are one and the same people. In many other respects, the American people are one; and the government which is alone capable of controlling and managing their interests in all these respects is the government of the Union....The people have declared, that in the exercise of all powers given for these objects it is supreme. It can, then, in effecting these objects, legitimately control all individuals or governments within the American territory. The constitution and laws of a state, so far as they are repugnant to the constitution and laws of the United States, are absolutely void. These states are constituent parts of the United States. They are members of one great empire—for some purposes sovereign, for some purposes subordinate. (19 US at 413–14)*

Marshall gives us a final guide to the question of state and federal relations and proper means of settling them, together with an implicit prediction of nature of the tempest that finally resolved the question of state versus federal supremacy that rocked the nation forty years later:

*These collisions may take place in times of no extraordinary commotion. But a constitution is framed for ages to come, and is designed to approach immortality as nearly as human institutions can approach it. Its course cannot always be tranquil. It is exposed to storms and tempests, and its framers must be unwise statesmen indeed, if they have not provided it, as far as nature will permit, with the means of self-preservation from the perils it may be destined to encounter. No government ought to be so defective in its organization as not to contain within itself the means of securing the execution of its own laws against other dangers than occur every day. (19 US at 387)*

The fact that the part (individual states) may not affect the whole (the United States) as a matter of Constitutional law does not mean that the whole may not enforce its will on the part. As in *Baker v Carr* in the discussion of voting, even matters which traditionally have been the subject of state control (such as apportionment for state legislative districts) may be subjected to federal intervention if the state action is deemed to be so outrageous as to constitute a denial of equal protection of the law, and thus a violation of the Fourteenth Amendment. Similarly, in *Fiske v Kansas* in applying the Bill of Rights, a state action may also be such as to deny a generally accepted right to an individual, and thus bring the state action within the Fourteenth Amendment prohibition against the denial of due process of law. In either situation, the Fourteenth Amendment would provide a basis for a review of a state's action by the United States government.

## INTERSTATE RELATIONS

Relations among the states are generally controlled by Article IV of the Constitution. The applications of some of the sections of Article IV are fairly well settled and easy to understand. For example, Section 2 provides that "The citizens of each state shall be entitled to all the privileges and immunities of citizens in the several states" (the **"Privileges and Immunities Clause"**). This has been interpreted to mean that if a state gives a privilege, such as the right to buy and sell property to all of its citizens, that state may not deny that privilege to out-of-state residents simply because they are from out of state. "But wait!" any college student who has investigated the phenomenon of out-of-state tuition for public universities will say. "What about the higher rate of tuition that I, a resident of Illinois, would have to pay to go to the University of Wisconsin at Madison?" That and similar discrimination against out-of-staters illustrates how the clause works. It is only a privilege which *every* resident of the state has that must be extended to residents of other states. Not every resident of Wisconsin goes to college, and thus higher rates of tuition for out-of-state residents is not a violation. Section 2 also contains the provision for extradition, which provides that a criminal fleeing from one state who is apprehended in another state " . . . shall, on demand of the executive authority of the state from which he fled, be delivered up . . . " which means just what it says.

Somewhat more difficult to understand is Section 1, which provides that, "Full faith and credit shall be given in each state to the public acts, records and judicial proceedings of every other state" (the "**Full Faith and Credit Clause**"). A great deal of confusion has grown up around this clause—how much credit to what sort of proceedings? Generally the textbook answer to the scope and effect of the Full Faith and Credit Clause is that all other states are bound by the finding of facts of the original state to deal with a particular matter, and then the other states are free only to apply their law to the already-determined facts. The reasoning behind this clause was set forth in *Sutton v Leib* (342 US 402 1952):

> . . . *Illinois' conclusion as to this claim for alimony must be reached under Illinois law on the basis of giving the various proceedings the effect to which the Constitution entitles them. In this way the Full Faith and Credit Clause performs its intended function of avoiding relitigation in other states of adjudicated issues, while leaving the law of the forum state the application of the predetermined facts to the new problem. (342 US at 497)*

That case gives an illustration of the operation of the Full Faith and Credit Clause, perhaps even to the operation of its outer limits. Mrs. Sutton had been divorced from Leib under Illinois law and received alimony under that divorce decree until she should re-marry. She married Henzel in a Nevada ceremony after Henzel had secured a Nevada divorce from Mrs. Henzel (unfortunately failing to serve Mrs. Henzel with notice that he was going to divorce her). Mrs. Henzel filed an action in New York for support, which Henzel resisted in the New York court. New York declared the Henzel's marriage valid and Mrs. Sutton's Nevada marriage "null and void" because, under United States law, you can only legally have one spouse at one time. Mrs. Sutton filed in Nevada for an annulment, which was granted (because Nevada was bound by the New York finding that the Henzels' original marriage was valid—a finding of fact conditioned by New York law, New York being the first state to determine the validity of *that* marriage).

The Nevada annulment of the Henzel-Sutton marriage was the result of applying Nevada law to the set of facts coming in from New York. Now Mrs. Sutton (who apparently hooked up with Sutton in holy matrimony at some time after the events noted above) is suing Leib for back alimony for the time between the ceremony with Henzel in Nevada (which caused Leib to stop paying alimony) and the finding that the marriage with Henzel was invalid (alternate claims are advanced for either the New York finding or the Nevada annulment.) The Supreme Court found that Illinois was stuck with the *fact* of an annulled marriage, but that Illinois would apply its own law to that fact to determine what further action should be taken:

> *Full faith and credit to the New York annulment, which is conclusive everywhere as to the marriage status of petitioner and Henzel, compels*

*Illinois to treat their Nevada marriage as void. The force of that rule, however, does not require that the effect of the New York annulment on rights incident to this declaration of the invalidity of the Nevada marriage ceremony shall be the same in all states....Illinois is free to decide for itself the effect of New York's declaration of annulment on the obligations of respondent, a stranger to that decree. (342 US at 409-10)*

Section 4 provides that "[t]he United States shall guarantee to each state a republican form of government . . . " (the "**Guarantee Clause**"). The Guarantee Clause in the Constitution is somewhat similar to the appendix in the human body: it's never used and no one knows what it was originally intended to do. When various cases came before the Supreme Court to enforce the Guarantee Clause, the Supreme Court declined to decide the case on the grounds that it was a political question. The Court reviewed the cases dealing with the Guarantee Clause in *Baker v Carr*, and cited the determining and enforcing authority for the clause as found by those prior decisions:

*Under this article of the Constitution it rests with Congress to decide what government is the established one in a State. For the United States to guarantee to each state a republican government, Congress must necessarily decide what government is established in the State before it can determine whether it is republican or not. And when the senators and representatives of a State are admitted into the councils of the Union, the authority of the government under which they are appointed, as well as its republican character is recognized by the proper constitutional authority. And its decision is binding on every other department of the government, and could not be questioned in a judicial tribunal. (369 US at 220, quoting Taney's opinion in* Luther v Borden*)*

# GETTING NEW STATES

Section 3 empowers Congress to set up the process for the admission of new states. Although there have been a few exceptions (Texas, for example, was admitted by a joint resolution of Congress because it had been an independent country since winning its revolution against Mexico at the Battle of San Jacinto), the process for admission or creation of a new state begins with the population of a United States territory petitioning Congress for admission to the Union as a new state. Congress has the absolute and unappealable authority to accept or reject the petition (and did a number of times when both Alaska and Hawaii petitioned for admission, as an example). If Congress approves of the petition for admission, it passes an enabling act authorizing the citizens of the territory to hold a constitutional convention for the purposes of writing a constitution for the new state-to-be. Congress may require that certain provisions be included in the new state constitution (e.g. Utah was required to include a provision in the constitution for its new state prohibiting polygamy). When the constitution is completed, it is submitted to Congress for its approval. Upon acceptance by Congress, the state is admitted as the latest of the United States.

# FORMS OF STATE GOVERNMENT

States each have their own state governments. Generally the state governments mimic the forms of the United States government to some degree. Sometimes the same names are used for some state government offices as are used for federal offices. An example would be state senators (and every state has them) who should not be confused with United States senators. Similarly, the Circuit Court of Cook County, Illinois (the lowest level of trial court in Illinois) should not be confused with a Circuit Court of Appeals in the federal court system (which is one notch below the United States Supreme Court). Despite the fact that we have fifty states and fifty state governments, there *are* some general observations which can be made.

Each of the states has its own state constitution which performs the same functions within a state as the U.S.Constitution performs for the entire country acting as a blueprint for the state government and setting up the state's version of civil rights and criminal defendants' rights. If there is a conflict between a state statute or constitution and any federal statute or the Constitution, the state provision is null and void.

Each of the states has a Chief Executive called the Governor, elected by the people. Most (not all) of the states have other elected officials of the Executive Branch, including the Lieutenant Governor (some states, such as Maine elect only the Governor, whereas Arizona elects all of the standard Executive Branch officials *except* the Lieutenant Governor). The Executive Branch officials, including elected officials, on the state level usually have much the same job titles as the President's Cabinet and in the main do pretty much the same kinds of things as their federal counterparts (e.g. the Secretary of Agriculture is concerned with growing things for money on both levels). A major exception is the Secretary of State. On the federal level he oversees the conduct of foreign affairs as his primary focus. On the state level the Secretary of State is the "miscellaneous" file of government, dealing with things as varied as driver's licenses, registering stocks and bonds and overseeing the operation of public libraries.

All states have legislatures—forty-nine of them with two chambers (Nebraska is unicameral, having only a Senate). Those states with two chambers all call one of them the Senate. The name for the other chamber will differ from state to state. The Senate within a state will usually have fewer members sitting for a longer time elected from larger districts than the other chamber. The relations between the Governor and the Legislature may be more complex than that of the President and Congress, as some states have given the Governor much greater veto authority than the President enjoys and some Legislatures possess the ability to remove Executive Branch and Judicial Branch officers by virtue of something called "**joint address**" (removal for strictly political reasons) without having to come up with the "high crimes and misdemeanors" kind of thing that impeachment usually requires on both levels.

Each state has its own judicial system with both trial courts and appellate courts. A major difference with the federal court system is that state court judges are typically elected and are thus subject to periodic review by the voters. Some states have a split (or bifurcated) system of appellate courts between courts of civil appeals and courts of criminal appeals. Most have a unitary system with intermediate appellate courts hearing appeals of both types. All states have a single highest court of appeals which hears both civil and criminal appeals as the final authority in the state judiciary (Maryland and New York call it the Court of Appeals, everyone else calls it the Supreme Court—New York calls its *trial* courts the Supreme Court, which can cause confusion if you're watching a New York-based courtroom drama).

In regard to the state equivalent to federalism (the relationship between the state government on the one hand and subordinate levels of government on the other) an important thing to recall is that local governments have no rights against their state governments. It is not necessary for a local government to commit a serious wrong (of the same level of objectionability as a state's wrongdoing necessary to invoke the Fourteenth Amendment) for a state government to override a local decision. Any local decision of any level of importance or discretion can be overridden by its state government. Thus local governments can be viewed as mere extensions of the state government, rather than independently functioning entities of their own.

# Chapter Exercises ❖ . . . and the States

Name_____Section_____

1.  Explain what happens if a state statute directly contra-
    dicts a federal statute and why.

2.  Explain the process whereby a territory becomes a
    state.

3.  Discuss some of the offices in state government that
    would be found in most states.

# CHAPTER SIX

# *Nominations, Elections and Voting*

*Chapter Objectives*

As a result of studying this chapter, the student should be able to perform the following activities:

1. Explain the distinguishing characteristics of elections in the United States when compared to elections held in other countries.
2. Explain the processes which could be used to get a candidate on the ballot.
3. Explain the operation of the amendments to the Constitution expanding the right to vote.
4. Explain the operation of the Voting Rights Act of 1965.

## ELECTIONS

The ultimate method which is employed to choose people to serve in office in both of the political branches, Congress and the President, is an election. The election which chooses the actual individuals who will sit in their respective seats of power in Washington is called the **general election**. It takes place in November of even-numbered years. (In writing this I am assuming that members of the House and Senate are around to serve out their full terms.) In the event that something untimely, such as death, intervenes to prevent a member of Congress from completing a term, then a temporary replacement is appointed usually by the governor of the member's state. If enough time remains of the member's term, then a **special election** is held for the unexpired portion of the term.

In the much more common general election situation, as we noted previously, members of the House of Representatives have terms of two years in length. Thus every general election is for all the seats in the House. Senators have six year terms, but those terms are staggered, so that every general election will see roughly one-third of the Senate seats being contested. Presidential terms are for four years, so *every other* general election for Congress will be a **Presidential election year**. (The non-Presidential general elections are usually called **off-year elections** because the big national office is not being contested.) The successor to the Presidency serves out the full remaining term so that there are no special elections to fill the unexpired term of office of a President who has been replaced. Most states key their general elections to the national general elections. Thus a November general election would have candidates for both state and federal offices. Local governments do not necessarily tie their elections to the November general elections. To use an example from right up the road from where I am sitting: Chicago's general election for mayor and the city council is held in April, while elections for Cook County,Illinois (the county in which Chicago is located) are held at the same time as the November general elections.

The fact that I can refer to "November general elections" illustrates a major difference between our system of government and the *parliamentary system* which most of the rest of the world's democracies use as their system. Under a parliamentary system, elections for the national legislature and national executive (the two are synonymous under a parliamentary system because the leader of the majority of the legislature *is* the head of the executive) are held whenever one of three alternatives comes to pass. One option is when the maximum term of office for a parliament has expired. Since the experience of England with the Long Parliament and its truncated version, the Rump Parliament which together lasted through the last part of the reign of Charles I, the English Civil War, the Protectorate of Oliver Cromwell and into the first portion of the reign of Charles II,[1] some outer limit for the duration of each Parliament has been set. When that outer limit of years is reached, national elections **must** be held (in Great Britain the limit is currently five years).

---

1.　*The Age of Reason Begins,* by Will and Ariel Durant. New York: Simon and Schuster (1961) 207–221;*The Age of Louis XIV,*by Will and Ariel Durant. New York:Simon and Schuster (1963) 183–204

The other two options that cause national elections under the parliamentary system are employed much more frequently. If the leader of the majority in parliament feels confident about winning national elections at any given time, he or she may dissolve parliament and hold national elections within a short time thereafter. With a new parliament and presumably a larger majority (if the leader has guessed right about the mood of the voters), the majority has another full parliamentary maximum term to work with.

At times the leader of a parliament is forced to dissolve parliament involuntarily. This is because a majority of the parliament has given the leader a *vote of "no confidence"*. Technically this means that a resolution has passed the legislature in which a majority of the parliament has voted that it "has no confidence in the leadership of the parliament any longer". This is where the term "no confidence vote" gets its name. Conversely, the "vote of confidence" expresses support for the leadership. (I should note that the term "vote of confidence" in parliamentary countries is just that—an affirmation of support for the leader. There is no flavor of being about ready to remove the leader which the phrase has taken on in this country).

An obvious result of the uncertainty of the timing of parliamentary elections—even the first alternative is a certain period, say five years, from the time the current parliament opened; the other two options are completely variable depending on the free choices made by the relevant individual since there are no fixed elections in a parliamentary system. We cannot talk about an equivalent to **the** November elections in Canada, for example, because national elections in Canada can happen at any time. Thus the **fixed** nature of general elections in the United States is a distinguishing factor of our system.

Another distinguishing factor is the fact that the elections are **periodic**. General elections in the United States will happen at the appointed time no matter what else is going on. As an example, even during our great national convulsion of the Civil War, with Lee's Army of Northern Virginia only a short distance from Washington, the Presidential election between Lincoln and MacClellan was held as scheduled. Indeed one of the alternative strategies of the Confederacy was to hope that "Little Mac" would win and a negotiated peace would leave Confederate independence intact.[2]

---

2.   Morison pp. 692–95

# CANDIDATES

So in the United States we have fixed, periodic general elections every November of even-numbered years to choose from among candidates for whatever national (and usually state and sometimes even local) offices need to be filled in that election. "Election" is what we call in logic a 'primitive term.' (In the words of Justice Potter Stewart of the Supreme Court in quite another context, "I may not be able to define it, but I know it when I see it.") The term **"candidate"** is defined in a number of ways in the federal statutes. Basically they all boil down to a candidate being one who sets himself up as being in the hunt for an office, whether (1) having his name printed on the official ballot for election; (2) seeking election by write-in vote; ( 2 USCA Section 381, having to do with contested Congressional elections); (3) taking the necessary steps to qualify for nomination or election; or (4) receiving, directly or indirectly, contributions to bring about nomination or election. (18 USCA Section 591, having to do with prohibiting certain political activities).

The first alternative means of deciding who is going to be designated as a candidate makes reference to "printed on the official ballot." This gives rise to the question just who is doing the printing of this "official ballot." The answer is that each state prepares and prints its own official ballots, thus the definition of how one qualifies as a candidate and what constitutes a political party are generally questions to be decided within each state by the law of that state. Typically it is how individuals get their names on ballots, both general election ballots and, where appropriate, direct primary ballots, is set up by state statute, subject to being occasionally overridden by superseding federal statutes, as is the case with the Voting Rights Act of 1965. "Getting names on ballots" includes both names which are *printed* on the ballot and how one goes about writing in a vote for a candidate who is not printed as one of the officially listed candidates.

# POLITICAL PARTIES

Since the states are spending their money for the (in total amount) expensive business of printing up ballots for elections, one of the aspects of state concern in regard to ballots is not wasting state time and money on frivolous candidates who are not, or should not be,serious in their candidacies. (An example of a frivolous candidacy would be, and I am not making this up, a hog named Pigasus who was the announced candidate of the Youth International Party in 1968).

In order to be sure that the candidates are serious and that printing their names on the ballot would not be a waste of state time and money, each state has defined not just what candidates are, but also what political parties are. States usually divide parties on the general election ballot into one of two types: **established parties** and **new parties**. An established party is one which received at least a certain minimum threshold percentage of votes in the last general election (or, in a few cases averaged a certain percentage of votes in the previous two general elections). The idea behind designating a group as an established political party is that it has shown sufficient support in previous elections and that it would not be a waste of the state's time and money to print that party's candidates on the general election ballot.

Similarly, new parties must also show sufficient support among voters that it would not be a waste of the state's time to list *its* candidates. Being new, these parties cannot show voter support through success in previous general elections, so the alternate method of showing support developed for new parties is through petition. A new party must secure a certain number of signatures of registered voters on a petition indicating that the signers will support the candidates of the proposed new party (obviously with the device of the secret ballot it is impossible to enforce this commitment in a general election). Usually the number of signatures required is expressed as a percentage of votes cast in the last general election, and usually there is a parallel between the number of signatures required on the petition for a new party on the one hand and the number of votes required in a general election to qualify as an established party on the other. (In the case of Pigasus mentioned above, the Youth International Party did not qualify as either an established party on the basis of votes won in the previous general election or as a new party based upon the number of signatures secured on a petition. Thus American voters did not have a chance to vote on a clear choice about pork barrel politics in 1968.)

# CAUCUS

Since officially recognized parties, whether new or established, get slots for each office contested in a general election, the question then becomes how, within a political party, a party's candidates are chosen as its representatives for the general election. Traditionally one of three modes for choice of a party's candidates is employed, depending on what state is under consideration. In terms of the order of development, the first method of selection of a party's candidates to be used was the **caucus**. This is a system whereby the leaders of a political party choose the candidates of that party for the offices to be contested at the next general election. The term for such a method is sometimes known these days in many states as nomination by committee.

Incidentally, some states (such as Iowa) reserve the term "caucus" for their method of expressing preference for presidential candidates and selecting delegates for the national presidential conventions of the Democrats and Republican. Such caucuses are complex in their execution, with a series of meetings of people wanting to participate and are best understood, like rankings of tennis professionals or scoring the decathlon, by experts in the field.

## DELEGATE CONVENTION

Obviously, being reserved for the party leaders, the mechanism of the caucus was not terribly democratic since the vast majority of party members were excluded from the process of choosing that party's candidates. As a part of the broadening of the electoral process that historians call "Jacksonian Democracy" (for President Andrew Jackson, who was viewed by his contemporaries as being swept into office by "King Mob")[3] , the selection process was made more democratic through the device of the **delegate convention**. In the delegate convention, members of a political party choose representatives from among themselves as delegates. These delegates then meet in a convention (hence the name) which chooses the party's candidates for the general election. This is clearly representative democracy, albeit indirect, and is essentially the same process employed in the election of members of the House of Representatives in concept.

## DIRECT PRIMARY

In its actual practice, the delegate convention came over time to be just as much an extension of party bosses as the caucus. Consequently, the reformers of the Progressive Party came up with the device of the **direct primary**, which our common usage has shortened to "primary." In a direct primary, members of a party vote directly to choose the candidates of the party for the general election. Some states only have a single primary, with the party's nominee

---

3 Morison pp. 422–26

being the candidate with the largest number of votes, even if it is less than a majority (as, for example, in a three-way race). Other states make provision for a second runoff election if no candidate got a majority of the votes in the first primary. In a runoff election the top two vote-getters square off, with the winner being assured a majority of the votes cast.

The device of the primary election also has ballots which are printed up at state expense, so the problem of assuring that only serious candidates are on the ballot has only been pushed back a notch. The question now becomes how to assure that the candidates for the primary ballot are serious. One common device is a **nominating petition**, essentially the same sort of thing as was required for a new party to get on the ballot for the general election. The state fixes the number of valid signatures of registered voters required to get on the primary ballot which is usually expressed as a certain percentage of the votes cast for that party in the last *primary* election. Obviously the number of votes cast for a single party in a primary election is probably going to be less than the total number of votes cast for all parties in a general election so that the number of votes determining the number of signatures required to get on a primary ballot is usually lower than the number of signatures required to be on the ballot as a new party. Getting the required number of signatures indicates at least the minimum base of voter support required to be a serious candidate.

Somewhat less frequently employed is the device of the **declaration of candidacy**, in which a candidate fills out a form to get on the primary ballot, but also puts down a large refundable deposit of money. If the candidate gets at least a low percentage of the votes in the primary (thereby proving to be a serious candidate) the money is returned and the state's time and money has not been wasted adding a frivolous candidate on the official ballot. If the threshold amount is not reached, suggesting that it was a frivolous candidacy, then the forfeited deposit not only penalizes the candidate, but also compensates the state for the wasted time and money.

# VOTING

The actual act of voting is how qualified citizens participate in the business of government. As has been noted elsewhere many times—if you didn't vote, don't complain. The importance of the right to vote in our system was cited by the Supreme Court as a basis for its decision in the voting rights case of *Louisiana v United States*, 380 US 128 (1965), wherein the Court determined that a suit to preserve the right to vote would proceed because

> *The allegations of this complaint were too serious, the right to vote in this country is too precious, and the necessity of settling grievances peacefully in the courts is too important for this complaint to have been dismissed. (380 US at 145)*

The importance of a fully equal right to vote was raised to a constitutionally protected level as was seen in the case of *Baker v Carr*. In *Baker* the United States Supreme Court expressed its view of the importance of the right to vote in our system of government, as that decision upheld the assertion that:

> *[lessening the effectiveness of an individual's right to vote] constitutes arbitrary and capricious state action, offensive to the [requirement that no state deny any person the equal protection of the laws imposed by the] Fourteenth Amendment in its irrational disregard of the standard of apportionment . . . effecting a gross disproportion of representation to the voting population. . . . A citizen's right to a vote free of arbitrary impairment by state action has been judicially recognized as a right secured by the Constitution, when such impairment resulted from dilution by a false tally . . . or by a refusal to count votes from arbitrarily selected precincts . . . or by a stuffing of the ballot box. . . . (369 US at 207–08)*

Note, incidentally, that this decision also recognizes that the circumstances surrounding the conduct of voting, nominations and elections will, in the absence of overriding Federal concern, be the subject of state action. The *Katzenbach* decision recognized the overall principle of state control of the voting process, subject to federal intervention in a few exceptional classes of cases, "As against *the reserved powers of the States* [emphasis added], Congress may use any rational means to effectuate the constitutional prohibition of racial discrimination in voting." (383 US at 324)

Some aspects of the right to vote are protected by the Constitution. The Fifteenth Amendment expanded the right to vote to all qualified male citizens, regardless of their race, color or "previous condition of servitude", i.e. the Fifteenth Amendment gave former male slaves constitutional protection of their right to vote. The Nineteenth Amendment gave women the right to vote, correcting an intentional omission by the drafters of the Fifteenth. The Twenty Fourth Amendment prohibited payment of any tax as a precondition for voting. The Twenty-Sixth Amendment lowered the minimum voting age from twenty-one to eighteen (under the stimulus of the Vietnam War and the slogan that "If they're old enough to fight, they're old enough to vote".)

# THE VOTING RIGHTS ACT OF 1965

As was noted in *Mapp v Ohio* and other criminal defendant rights cases, a right without a means of enforcing that right ("a right without a remedy" to use the construction of some early decisions and commentators) is mere words, the same as having no right at all. Although Congress made a number of attempts to pass legislation to protect the right to vote given by the Fifteenth Amendment, its efforts were largely unsuccessful until the passage of the Voting Rights Act of 1965.

The Voting Rights Act of 1965, like all of its voting rights acts predecessors, was based on the authority given to Congress to enforce the extension of the franchise to men of all races in the Fifteenth Amendment. After extending the right on Section 1 of the Amendment, Congress took note of the problem of providing a "right without a remedy" noted above as well as the already existing efforts of the South to reverse the "verdict of Appomattox" by restoring the effects of slavery without the name through a series of state-by-state enactments called collectively, the "Black Codes." The effect of the Black Codes was to restore former slaves to their position of a powerless labor force, prohibited from taking any action either individually or collectively to better their social or economic status. The Reconstruction Congress thus provided itself and its successors with authorization of "power to enforce this article by appropriate legislation" in Section 2 of the Fifteenth Amendment.

After the 1876 Presidential Election, in which the Republicans took the disputed Tilden-Hayes contest, federal troops were removed from the last of the occupied states of the former Confederacy and those states were largely left to the undisturbed regulation of their internal affairs until the middle of this century. A series of statutes attempted to assure the right to vote for all in the South, but the entrenched powers in the governments of the former Confederate states took a series of inventive moves to nullify each attempt.

Against this background of move and countermove, Congress passed the Voting Rights Act of 1965. An excellent overview of the steps provoking the passage of the Voting Rights Act, together with examples of the worst instances of abuse, is given in the opinion in *South Carolina v Katzenbach*,383 US 300 (1966) which found the Voting Rights Act of 1965 to be a proper and constitutional exercise of legislative power under Section 2. The Supreme Court summed up its assessment of the background of the Act thusly:

*The Voting Rights Act was designed by Congress to banish the blight of racial discrimination in voting, which has infected the electoral process in parts of our country for nearly a century. The Act creates stringent new remedies for voting discrimination where it persists on a pervasive scale, and in addition the statute strengthens existing remedies for pockets of voting discrimination elsewhere in the country. (383 US at 308)*

After an extensive recitation of the offenses discussed above (as examples, a white applicant passing the literacy test by writing "FRDUM FOOF SPETGH" while African-Americans with bachelor's and master's degrees were held to have failed the requirement of explaining a section of the state constitution to the satisfaction of the registrar (383 US at 312), the Court sketched the outline of the provisions of the Voting Rights Act by stating that

*The heart of the Act is a complex scheme of stringent remedies aimed at areas where voting discrimination has been most flagrant. Section 4(a)–(d) lays down a formula defining the States and political subdivisions to which these new remedies apply. The first of these remedies . . . is the suspension of literacy tests and similar voting qualifications for a period of five years from the last occurrence of substantial voting discrimination. Section 5 prescribes a second remedy, the suspension of all new voting regulations pending review by federal authorities. . . . The third . . . is the assignment of federal examiners . . . to list qualified voters who are thereafter entitled to vote. . . . Other provisions . . . appointment of federal poll watchers . . . excuse those made eligible to vote from paying past poll taxes . . . provides for balloting by persons denied access to the polls in areas where federal examiners have been appointed . . . broadly prohibits the use of voting rules to abridge exercise of the franchise on racial grounds [this was amended in 1982 to provide for prohibition of rules having the effect of racial discrimination, not just rules which can be proven to have been motivated by an intent to so discriminate] . . . excuses citizens educated in American schools from passing English-language literacy tests. (383 US at 315–16)*

The application of these various remedies essentially outlawed the devices which yielded the worst abuses and provided for conducting the registration and actual polling process under the eyes of federal examiners empowered to seize control of either or both processes for the purposes of conducting the election. This latter federal operation was to forestall any further creative devices on the part of discriminatory authorities ("Just in case you think of something that we didn't think of, we'll reserve an authority to override any racially discriminatory action you might come up with.")

The provisions of the Act concerned with banning voting qualification tests are triggered either by: 1) a finding by the Attorney General,published in the *Federal Register*, that such discriminatory conduct had been carried out in a state or subdivision thereof as part of a pattern of discrimination; or 2)the Director of the Census determines that less than 50% of its voting age citizens were registered to vote. Although the finding by the Attorney General is not appealable itself, the imposition of the corrective measures of the Act can be prevented by a judgment from the District Court of the District of Columbia that discriminatory devices *had not*, contrary to the Justice Department findings, been used to limit the right to vote on racial grounds during the preceding five years.

Similarly, a finding by the Attorney General will cause federal examiners to descend to observe and, if necessary, seize control of the voting process. Either a finding from the Attorney General himself or by the District Court for the District of Columbia is required to terminate their visit. Thus the Act permits corrective action on the part of the federal government and then allows time to pass while an affected unit of subnational government must see time pass while pursuing its available remedies of appeal. This reverses the near-century in which the attempt to correct an abuse (which before the Voting Rights Act was done on an individual-by-individual basis) could be implemented because the locality's appeals had to be fully exhausted *before* any such implementation.

## Chapter Exercises ❖ Nominations, Elections and Voting

Name_____Section_____

1. Explain the different ways available for a candidate to become the nominee of an established party in a general election. (This means that you will have to define "candidate", "established party" and "general election" as you explain the various ways available.)

2. Explain how the Voting Rights Act of 1965 was enacted to provide a remedy to enforce the expansions of the right to vote accomplished by the amendments to the Constitution concerned with voting.

# CHAPTER SEVEN

# *Defense and Foreign Policy*

### Chapter Objectives

As a result of studying this chapter, the student should be able to perform the following activities:

1. Define the term "nation-state" and discuss its activities.
2. Explain the structure and problems of the United Nations.
3. Explain the difference between defense and diplomacy.
4. Explain the difference between an executive agreement and a treaty.
5. Explain fully the potential confrontation between the Congress and the President created by the War Powers Resolution of 1973.

---

**"War is a continuation of politics by other means"**

*Karl von Clausewitz*

**"Political power grows out of the barrel of a gun"**

*Mao Zedong*

# NATION-STATES

Defense and foreign policy are twisted together in such a way as to be impossible to separate. This is because the final authority in diplomatic negotiations between nations will always be force if all else fails. The basic unit in foreign relations is the nation, or more technically, **nation-state** (a nation being any group of people that call themselves a nation, the term "nation-state" indicating that this group is politically free to act on its own as a separate country, without any higher level of government being able to force compliance to that other authority's decision).

Internationally each nation-state decides things for itself and takes action based on its own decisions. The only way that a nation-state's conduct can be changed without changing the mind of the nation-state is through sheer force (note that a nation-state can be *persuaded* to alter its course of action, but then the nation-state is making up its own mind). Persuading a nation-state is diplomacy—forcing a nation-state is defense (or, in the more accurate label used before this century's preoccupation with looking nice—war). When these activities are carried on with regard to countries other than our own, diplomacy is usually called "foreign relations", with the Department of State being the Cabinet Department concerned with it. Defense is the subject of concern of the Defense Department. (An image which it is useful to keep in mind in looking at defense and diplomacy questions on the international scene is that of three-year-olds playing in a sandbox: virtually every activity internationally will have a parallel function carried out in the sandbox, and the source of final authority in a decision will, in both cases, be either threatened or applied force.)

# INTERNATIONAL ORGANIZATIONS

Despite the fact that each nation-state decides things for itself (and will carry through with its decision in the absence of greater force being applied by an outside nation-state), there are a vast number of world or international organizations which seek to bind all or parts of the nation-states in the international community together for general or limited special purposes. The problem with international organizations is that they are essentially voluntary in nature: if Nation A does not want to go along with the decision imposed by a world organization, there is nothing short of war that the other nations of the organization can bring to bear to force compliance aside, of course, from expelling Nation A from the voluntary organization (our three-year-olds at the sandbox refuse to play with one of their number who has offended in some way, Although this may hurt his feelings, it is not really forcing him to change his ways.)

A typical example of a voluntary organization would be the United Nations. There are, at this writing, more than 150 members of the UN. The organization has a General Assembly, where each member-nation has one vote and issues are debated and voted on. Isolation or casting out of offending members is used to punish wrong-doers.

The Security Council has seventeen members. They carry out actions which the Council (note that this is *not* the Assembly doing the deciding) determines should be done. Of the seventeen members of the Council, twelve are selected by the General Assembly and five (the United States, Great Britain, France, Russia and the People's Republic of China) are permanent by virtue of winning World War II and founding the UN. Each of the five permanent members of the Security Council has an absolute veto over any proposed action which the Security Council and the UN may take. Conversely, all five permanent members must agree together before the UN can do anything.

Finally, the UN has a branch called the Secretariat, which includes both the office of the Secretary General and a number of specialized agencies. The Secretary General makes arrangements for carrying out decisions of the Security Council and General Assembly, but this is more like paying for things and making sure that they arrive at the right place at the right time instead of actually taking significant steps to enforce those decisions. (The Secretary General is not an executive in the sense of our President carrying out the laws passed by Congress.)

The various international agencies within the Secretariat are organized around a particular subject that they act upon (in this they are like our Cabinet Departments) but unlike our departments, the agencies cannot really enforce their decisions on a member which does not want to go along since that membership in each of these organizations is *voluntary* and the worst thing that can happen to the rogue member, short of the other members going to war, is to be expelled. (Again, if the international equivalent of hurt feelings is not going to change the wrong-doer's mind, it will continue to misbehave). International organizations under the umbrella of the Secretariat are thus largely confined to passing out information and providing technical advice and assistance to those nations willing to accept it. These agencies range from the extremely successful, UNICEF, to the largely futile, UNESCO.

The United Nations does not have a branch that is the equivalent of our judicial branch. There is a World Court which sits in the Hague in the Netherlands and which predates the UN, but the name "Court" is really a misnomer; really all that the World Court does is to arbitrate disputes between parties which both agree to submit themselves to its jurisdiction and then voluntarily abide by the terms of its decision. The World Court does not have the power to compel the attendance of the defendant and then enforce the decision it makes upon the loser. (It was this power to compel attendance and enforce decisions which defined which court in the United States system had jurisdiction of the person over the defendant).

The difficulty that the World Court has in enforcing its decisions shows the problems which any international organization faces in trying to conduct its business: the fundamental independence of each nation-state, be it member or non-member. There is little that can be done other than going to war to enforce a decision made by a world organization, and the decision of going to war is one of the utmost severity because people die in a war.

The question still remains, how does such an organization do its work? International organizations, having no power to impose a tax, must *ask* members to contribute the money necessary to carry out its day-to-day activities. If a member-nation does not contribute all or a portion of its dues, the organization has to either ask the other members to take up the slack or has to make do with less. Even if a question were to be so serious as to require military action, the organization would have to ask members to send troops and supply them voluntarily, since there is no power to compel military service or materiel for the organization.

# TREATIES

Aside from the ongoing international organizations, nation-states will make agreements between themselves without creating a separate on-going organization to carry out the terms of the agreement. We will refer to these as "treaties" here, although there are a number of forms of such agreements which are not formal treaties—chief among them in American foreign policy are executive agreements. A **treaty** can be thought of as a voluntary agreement between two or more nation-states, each of which agrees that it will do something. The treaty continues in effect so long as all parties continue to want to comply with its terms calling for particular action. Whenever one or more parties to the treaty stop wanting to perform its terms, the party or parties can simply stop complying and there is nothing aside from variations of isolation and war which can be applied to force compliance. As a matter of practicality, breaking of treaties is much more frequently the cause of war than refusing to follow the decision of an international organization, because treaties are frequently made to stop fighting between nation-states, and breaking a treaty that created peace almost certainly at least contemplates war as a possible result. Please note that the *only* thing that keeps a nation-state in compliance with a treaty is its own desire to follow it. Thus, it is as enforceable as a diet or quitting smoking or some other bad habit. If you want to break whatever pledge concerning personal behavior that has been made, there is nothing but your own conscience to stop you.

# WAR

As we have seen, the only thing which can enforce a decision on a nation-state is war. From the standpoint of our own country, we should consider what it is that is a war. In the time leading up to the Persian Gulf War, President Bush made frequent reference to the fact that the United States had been in more than three hundred wars in its history (some estimates go as high as almost four hundred—the difference being whether you classify a number of our conflicts with Native Americans as one war or several) with only five of those wars being declared by Congress (the War of 1812, Mexican-American War, Spanish-American War, World War I and World War II). This naturally leads to the question, "What is a war?" The Supreme Court in *Bas v Tingy* defined a war essentially as something which everyone knows is a war even if it is undeclared. For our present purposes, let us define a war as something in which our people in uniform are officially ordered to shoot at other people.

The next question which would follow would be, "How can we have a war which is undeclared?" The answer lies in the terms of Article I and Article II of the Constitution. Article I gives the Congress the power to *declare* war, and Article II gives the President the power to *make* war. The confusion of the split in the war powers is also present in the sections of the Constitution concerning the conduct of business in foreign relations. The President makes treaties with other countries, but the Senate must approve those treaties by a 2/3 margin if they are to become effective. The President, as we have seen before, has the power to receive ambassadors of another country (and thereby officially acknowledge the legal existence of that government), but it is the Senate that approves the nomination of *our* ambassadors to other countries. From a practical standpoint, the Congress must appropriate money to pay for all actions the United States takes, including actions of diplomacy and war.

The question of which will should control in the arena of foreign policy and whether Congress or the President should have the final say in questions of war and peace has never been answered in the case of a direct conflict between Congress on the one hand and the President on the other. The question of which should prevail is one of great concern even after more than two hundred years, because Congress passed the War Powers Resolution in 1973. Its constitutionality has not yet been tested. The War Powers Resolution seems to clearly contemplate direct Congressional limitation on the power of the President to make war. Let us look at the two cases which give the President the broadest grants of power in diplomacy and war, respectively.

# PRESIDENTIAL POWER IN FOREIGN RELATIONS

The case which gave an almost unlimited grant of power to the President in foreign relations is *United States v Curtiss-Wright Export Corporation,* 299 US 304 (1936). The case grew out of an attempt to fine the Curtiss-Wright Corporation for the attempted sale in 1934 of fifteen machine guns to Bolivia in violation of a Presidential proclamation prohibiting the sale of weapons to either Bolivia or its opponent in a border war, Paraguay. The proclamation was issued by FDR based on a joint resolution passed by Congress that same day. Curtiss-Wright contended that with the grant of power to the President, Congress was giving away too much power. By giving the power to decide about whether the proclamation should issue without putting any limitations on how the President should be making his decision about an embargo, Curtiss-Wright urged that Congress had given away the power to legislate, which was a violation of the Constitution's grant in Article I of the power to legislate to Congress and Congress alone.(This is similar to the question of requiring "clear guidelines" in the enabling acts that set up the various administrative agencies).

The Supreme Court found that it was not necessary for Congress to make a grant of power to decide whether or not to impose an embargo of arms sales to the two warring nations. The President is the sole judge of what to do in diplomatic questions by virtue of his position as head of a sovereign state, (essentially that the President had the power to decide how to proceed in diplomatic affairs by virtue of his position as successor to George III of England.)

The Supreme Court finding this great power for the President in foreign affairs at a time in history when it was cutting back on the grants of powers in the New Deal is the result of a sharp line which the Court drew between the exercise of power in external and in internal affairs. In internal actions, the President and Congress are merely exercising the powers which the states had exercised in dealing with their citizens after the Declaration of Independence. (The states took the power to legislate with regard to their citizens from England and each then exercised this power of internal regulation within its borders.) The Constitution merely took some of the powers which the states had to legislate internally and transmitted it to the central national government when the Constitution was ratified.

The power of conducting foreign relations, however, did not pass to the states separately when independence was taken. It passed from England to the new entity called the United States, without being parcelled out among the original thirteen because the United States was *a* new nation, *not* thirteen new nations. As a single new nation, the United States was a sovereign nation-state. As a sovereign nation-state, the new country had the sole power to decide for itself questions of war and peace, treaties and alliances. It is this ability to decide questions for itself in the realm over the national border that defines a sovereign nation-state. Since the power to decide foreign questions did not pass to the states, the states could not transmit the power to decide such questions later via the Constitution. Since the power was not transmitted through the Constitution, the power to decide questions of war and peace or international agreements was not subject to the limitations imposed by the Constitution.

This vast and unfettered (by either the Constitution or laws passed under its authority) power implied by national sovereignty means that someone must make the decisions that answer the question raised in external affairs. The Court in *Curtiss-Wright*, after noting that the power to decide meant that someone was going to have to do the deciding, determined that because the President was given the power to *make* treaties and agreements which are then subject to advice and consent from the Senate the President's will was to be supreme in questions of external policy. The Congress might, after the fact, decide against a deal that the President had made, but neither the Congress as a whole nor the Senate as a part of the Congress, had the power to interfere in the actual making of a deal. Further, the Court noted, the President has sources of information which are not available to either the public at large or Congress. Any attempt to dispute a President's suggestions in regard to a foreign policy should be made only *after* realization and consideration of the possibility that the President probably knows best and certainly knows more. Thus the President must be given much greater latitude—nearly unlimited—in external questions compared to internal decisions if " . . . embarrassment—perhaps serious embarrassment—is to be avoided and success for our aims achieved . . . ." (299 U.S. at 320)

# PRESIDENTIAL POWER TO MAKE WAR

Practically unlimited power to decide questions of war and peace is granted to the President by the case of *Martin v Mott* 25 US 19 (1827). Mott was seeking to recover goods which Martin, a deputy marshall, had seized to satisfy a fine that had been imposed on Mott. Mott had failed to report for duty when the New York state militia had been called out in 1814 pursuant to the commands of the governor. A court martial had fined Mott when it finally was convened and decided the issue in 1818. Mott urged that his property be returned because the New York militia was not needed in the conflict, as was shown by the fact that it was never ordered anywhere. Since the militia was not needed, Mott reasoned, the call up was not necessary and Mott should not be penalized for not engaging in a useless exercise.

The Supreme Court paid the greatest attention to the fact that the Congressional authority for calling out the militia was written in terms of " . . . suppress[ing] insurrections and repel[ling] invasions . . . ." (25 US at 28-9) and noted that Congress had given the power to take actions to defeat invasion or rebellion to the President in a statute passed in 1795.

The Supreme Court extended the power to actively resist ongoing invasions to include the power to take actions to prevent an invasion before the enemy crossed the border, "One of the best means to repel invasion is to provide the requisite force for action before the invader himself has reached the soil." (25 US at 29)

The Court then pointed out that the power to call up troops to repel invasion was necessarily a "limited" power—someone would have to *decide* whether the time was ripe for calling out the troops. The President would be, as the Constitutionally created Commander in Chief, the individual empowered to determine whether the situation demanded that the troops be called out. Such a decision would, by its very nature be triggered by an emergency. In an emergency of this type (a "sudden emergency" caused by "imminent danger" to use the language of the opinion) "prompt and unhesitating obedience to orders is indispensable to the complete attainment of the object." (25 US at 30) No one has the power to refuse to obey the orders, or even to pause and second guess the wisdom of the orders, because the war might be lost while soldiers were trying to figure out whether to obey the orders of their superiors.

Aside from the grant of power from Congress to the President by the Act of 1795, the power of Commander in Chief would render the President's decision absolutely final:

> . . . *[T]he authority to decide whether the exigency has arisen, belongs exclusively to the President, and that his decision is conclusive upon all other persons . . . .The law does not provide for any appeal from the judgment of the President . . . (25 US at 29,31)*

# THE WAR POWERS RESOLUTION

The vast grants of the power to decide questions of foreign relations and war and peace given in *Curtiss-Wright* and *Mott* would seem to fly in the face of the War Powers Resolution, enacted by Congress in 1973. The first thing to notice about the War Powers Resolution is that it is a *resolution*, not a law which has gone through the steps set forth in Article I about how a bill becomes a law. Assuming that the resolution is deemed to have effect even if it does not rise to the dignity of a statute, the apparent collision of the Resolution with the powers found by the Supreme Court in *Curtiss-Wright* and *Mott* would seem to set up a potential challenge either to the Resolution or the case law decisions. The Resolution states its case in its opening section,

> *It is the purpose of this chapter to fulfill the intent of the framers of the Constitution of the United States and insure the collective judgment of both the Congress and the President will apply to the introduction of United States Armed Forces into hostilities . . . (50 USCA Section 1541 (a))*

The attempt to assert Congressional power to affect decisions of war and peace are grounded in Article I Section 8 Clause 18, the Elastic Clause, which empowers Congress to enact laws not only to carry into effect all of its own enumerated powers, " . . . but also all powers vested by the Constitution in the Government of the United States, or in any department or officer thereof." (50 USCA Section 1541(b) Congress brings its own interpretation of the powers of the President as Commander-in-Chief as those:

> . . . *exercised only pursuant to (1) a declaration of war, (2) specific statutory authorization, or (3) a national emergency created by attack upon the United States, its territories or possessions, or its armed forces. (50 USCA Section 1541(c))*

In order to avoid the sort of problem envisioned by *Mott*, that of everyone sitting around and waiting to come to a final decision about whether military action by the United States is required, the Resolution sets up a period within which the President may exercise his authority as Commander-in-Chief without questions being raised to stop the application of force. When the disposition of United States forces abroad are such as to be introduced into hostilities or are placed so as to be likely to engage in hostile action, the President must report that fact to the Speaker of the House and President pro tempore of the Senate.(50 USCA Section 1543(a)) When such a report is submitted (or required to be submitted), a sixty day countdown begins. (50 USCA Section 1544 (b)) If Congress has not taken some affirmative legislative action in support of the military activity during that sixty day period (declaration of war, resolution in support of the action, resolution extending the sixty days) then the President has thirty more days within which to bring the troops home. Section 1544 (c) would seem to go even further in limiting the President's authority as a commander by requiring the President to remove troops from overseas at any time that Congress calls for that action by concurrent resolution.

## WHAT IS A WAR ?

Although the War Powers Resolution would seem to be in direct opposition to the *Mott* decision, some authority for the power of Congress to set limits of foreign military action can be found in the early decision of *Bas v Tingy*, 4 US 37 (1800) which dealt with the question, when is a war a properly constituted war?

In *Bas*, the plaintiff owned a cargo ship that had been captured by the French and then recaptured by U.S. naval forces. At the time a statute was in force that provided that owners of ships recaptured from "enemies" had to pay the rescuers 1/2 the value of the ship as a reward. The United States and Napoleonic France had been engaged in an on-going but undeclared war between their navies, with ships on both sides being boarded and seized, indeed both France and the United States commissioned what are called "privateers" (sort of bounty hunters on the high seas who were given official authority to engage in plunder of the other side).

It seemed that something involving blood and gunpowder was going on between the two sides, but if not a declared war as provided for by the Constitution, what was it? The answer that the justices of the Supreme Court agreed upon was that it was a war, but an **"imperfect"** war. A declared war, a **"perfect war"**, was one in which the population of one country was: given the authority to attack any of the citizens of the other, or in the words of Justice Washington

*... all the members of the nation declaring war are authorized to commit hostilities against all the members of the other, in every place, and under every circumstance (4 US at 40)*

The action against the French was much more limited in kind, with certain designated representatives of the United States being authorized by Congress to prey upon certain designated potential victims of the other side. The Supreme Court took a practical view of the status of the American and French forces "If they were not our enemies, I know not what constitutes an enemy," stated Justice Washington. Thus early on in our history the concept of fighting an undeclared war was considered, with authority for determining the existence and extent of hostilities residing with Congress. This great power of Congress would seem to be a source of authority for Congressional participation in decisions of war and peace.

# EXECUTIVE AGREEMENTS

The expansion of Congressional authority that history grants in *Bas* is matched by the expansion of the President's authority to conclude agreements with other governments *without* Congressional, specifically Senatorial, agreement—an expansion that was accomplished in the case of *U.S. v Belmont*, 301 US 324 (1937).

In *Belmont* the national government was seeking to recover assets deposited with the private bank of the Belmont family by a pre-Revolutionary Russian company. Stalin had asserted the legal title to the funds decades later, and then had given the rights to the money as a part of the settlement whereby the Soviet Union was recognized by FDR recall that the power to recognize another government, declare that it officially and legally exists so far as the United States is concerned, is a Presidential power implied by the Article II grant of the express power to "receive ambassadors."

The estate of August Belmont was contending that New York state law, which did not recognize seizure of funds in the United States by foreign revolutionary governments, should control. The U.S. replied that the existence of an agreement between Washington and Moscow created a national law which should control in a conflict with New York law. The Belmont forces returned that the only valid kind of international agreement was a treaty, which the agreement between FDR and Stalin obviously was not, as there had been no Senatorial advice and consent. The Supreme Court found that not only was the agreement between the heads of state of the United States and the Soviet Union superior to New York state law, but one which was as effective as a treaty, without requiring " . . . the participation of the Senate" (301 US at 331).

Further, the Supreme Court decided that the President was the only one to decide the terms and conditions of what have come to be called **executive agreement**. The importance of this sole power of the Executive branch to enter into such types of binding international agreements can be seen when you realize that there are many times as many executive agreements as treaties, with the total running into the tens of thousands.

## Chapter Exercises ❖ Defense and Foreign Policy

Name_____Section_____

1. Explain why the War Powers Resolution may involve a clash between the powers exercised by Congress and the President as a matter of constitutional law.

2. Explain why the concept of a nation-state will frustrate the operation of international organizations.

# Chapter Eight

# *Rights*

## RIGHTS AND THE STATES

The Constitution is the primary source of protection of the rights of individuals. Rights may be divided into two sorts: civil rights (those which everyone enjoys all the time, like freedom of speech) and defendants' rights (those which only become important when you are or are likely to become a defendant in a crime, like the right not to be forced to incriminate yourself). Most of the rights of individuals are said to be protected by the Bill of Rights, the first ten amendments to the Constitution. Thus we speak of freedom of speech as a "*First Amendment* right" and refusing to incriminate oneself as "standing on the *Fifth Amendment.*"

An initial hurdle which rights must get by is the language of the Bill of Rights, since each of the first eight amendments begins with the phrase, "*Congress* shall make no law . . . "

The question immediately arises whether the states are also prevented from taking actions which infringe on rights granted by the Bill of Rights. For more than a century the answer was affirmative. Even though the national government was prevented from attacking the rights of the individual, the states were under no such limitation.

The decision in *Fiske v Kansas* , 274 US 380 (1927) started a long process of assuring that the states were subject to the Bill of Rights as well as the federal government. In *Fiske* the defendant was charged with the crime of "criminal syndicalism", which made it a crime to advocate the overthrow of the government by violence. Fiske was an organizer for the International Workers of the World. (The IWW is more familiarly referred to in the literature of the time as "the Wobblies") Although Fiske and the Wobblies were guilty of suggesting that society was stacked against the worker and was grinding down the poor in a brutal fashion, they at no time advocated violence as a means of remedying social injustice. Fiske was convicted nonetheless, even though the state did not introduce a*ny* evidence that indicated that Fiske did anything in violation of the Kansas statute. Indeed,the only evidence brought forth in the trial was on the side of the defendant.

The U.S. Supreme Court found this conviction to be a violation of the Fourteenth Amendment (one of the so-called "War Amendments" passed in the wake of the Civil War) which stated that states could not deprive citizens of their liberty or property without "due process of law." The Supreme Court held that the finding of guilt "without evidence to support it . . . " (274 US at 385) was clearly a denial of a federal right—the federal right of due process. The Fourteenth Amendment was both the origin of the right of due process and the means whereby that right was applied to the states.

Over the remainder of the Twentieth Century, other rights have been found to be so fundamental that an infringement of one of these rights by a state has been held to constitute a denial of due process, a violation of the Fourteenth Amendment by the state. On a case by case, right by right basis, most of the Bill of Rights have eventually been applied to the states indirectly through the Fourteenth Amendment.

# THE ESTABLISHMENT CLAUSE

The beginning of the Bill of Rights, the first lines of the First Amendment, states that "Congress" and by extension the states (we'll only remind you again of the two step process if it becomes necessary to the discussion hereafter) "shall make no law respecting the establishment of religion . . . ." Immediately we are in territory which requires interpretation because the language of the Bill of Rights prohibits not just establishing a national religion, but even doing anything related to, "respecting", such an establishment.

This phrase has been called the **"Establishment Clause"** for two hundred years . There have been many different interpretations of the meaning of "respecting" over that previous two hundred years. There are two major interpretations of the meaning of the Establishment Clause. One is that there can be no interaction between government on the one hand and religion on the other in any way, shape or form (traced back to Thomas Jefferson, this is sometimes called "Jefferson's Chinese Wall of separation"). The other position is that government can deal with religions generally so long as it does not single any one religion out for favor over the others. Most court cases that have dealt with the issue have adopted a position between these two with a tendency to lean toward the latter.

The question of what is a religion was considered in the case of *United States v Ballard*, 322 US 78 (1944) which dealt with the mail fraud conviction of members of the Ballard family, who were the founders of the "I am" religious movement. The Ballards took their authority to heal the sick, curable and incurable, from the late Guy Ballard. Guy Ballard had claimed to be the Count of St. Germaine (a courtier with Louis XIII and Louis XIV), George Washington, and Jesus. He was the self-appointed "ascertained master", "divine messenger" and "divine entity". Particularly in view of the deceased status of Guy Ballard, the validity of the doctrine of the church of "I am" was called into question at trial, but the Supreme Court noted that no one should sit in judgment of the truth or falsity of any religion:

> *The religious doctrines espoused by the respondents might seem incredible, if not preposterous, to most people. But if those doctrines are subject to trial before a jury charged with finding their truth or falsity, then the same can be done with the religious beliefs of any sect. When the triers of fact undertake that task, they enter a forbidden domain. (322 US at 87)*

The Supreme Court tied freedom of religion to freedom of thought and noted that, if any religion was put to the test of objective and absolute proof, no religion was safe:

*Freedom of thought, which includes freedom of religious belief, is basic in a society of free men . . . .It embraces the right to maintain theories of life and death and of the hereafter which are rank heresy to followers of the orthodox faiths. Heresy trials are foreign to our Constitution. Men may believe what they cannot prove. They may not put to the proof their religious doctrines or beliefs. Religious experiences which are as real as life to some may be incomprehensible to others. (322 US at 86)*

To emphasize the fact that anyone could be hurt if their religion was put to the standards of the "I am" religion, the Supreme Court imagined what would happen if Christianity were put to a trial by jury:

*Many take their gospel from the New Testament. But it would hardly be supposed that they could be tried before a jury charged with the duty of determining whether those teachings contained false representations. The miracles of the New Testament, the Divinity of Christ, life after death, the power of prayer are deep in the religious convictions of many. If one could be sent to jail because a jury in a hostile environment found those teachings false, little indeed would be left of religious freedom. The Fathers of the Constitution were not unaware of the varied and extreme views of religious sects, of the violence of disagreement among them, and of the lack of any one religious creed on which all men would agree. They fashioned a charter of government which envisaged the widest possible toleration of conflicting views. Man's relation to his God was made no concern of the state. (322 US at 87)*

In the final analysis, the test of a religion is at first one of belief, before any other inquiry is made. In the words of the jury instructions of District Court, which was upheld by the decision in *Ballard:*

*The question of the defendants' good faith is the cardinal question in this case. . . . The jury will be called upon to pass on the question of whether or not the defendants honestly and in good faith believed the representations set forth in the indictment, . . . or whether these representations were mere pretenses without honest belief on the part of the defendants. (322 US at 82)*

# THE LEMON v KURTZMAN TEST

The leading case in this area, which establishes the test applied by all subsequent cases, is *Lemon v Kurtzman* ,403 US 603 (1970). That case involved statutes passed by Pennsylvania and Rhode Island which were designed to pay a supplement to the salaries of teachers in private schools. Each state had enacted stringent reporting requirements to make absolutely certain that no state monies were going to anyone who taught religion so as to assure that there was no state support of religion through supporting teachers of theology in private religious schools. Reports were required of teachers as to the subjects they taught and texts they used. The state would send people in to each school to examine the records of the school to make doubly sure that the requirements were being met.

The Supreme Court in *Lemon* set forth a three-step test to determine whether a state is in violation of the Establishment Clause.

1. The statute [or other governmental action] must have a secular [non-religious] purpose.

2. The primary effect of the statute must neither advance nor inhibit [help or hurt] religion;

3. The statute must not create "an excessive government entanglement with religion" [must not have government and religion mixed together too much]. This last is a judgment call on the part of the reviewing court. Clearly *some* government mixture with religion is acceptable, look at "In God We Trust" on your money. In order to be acceptable, the statute must get the right answer to each question.

The way this test is applied can be seen through its application to the facts in *Lemon* itself.

1. Does the statute have a non-religious purpose? Yes, the public has an interest in assuring that the parochial school system remains viable; otherwise, there would be too great an influx of students into the public school system for that system to handle. If there is a need for the parochial system to continue, there is also a need to assure that its graduates are educated. This in turn would suggest paying its teachers enough to live on. The level of pay for parochial school teachers had not been a problem when most parochial teachers were members of religious orders under a vow of poverty. The decline in the numbers of the teaching orders parochial schools were forced to hire lay teachers on the open market with inadequate wages and lower standards to teach. Increasing the total pay received by parochial school teachers to a competitive level would presumably attract better qualified teachers.

2. The statute must neither help nor hurt religion. Here a system of extensive reports and audits was created to make sure that there would be no contact between religion and anyone receiving the supplement.

3.  The statute must not create "excessive entanglement" between government and religion. Here is where the Pennsylvania and Rhode Island statutes fail, for the very reports created to assure that there is no state money going to religion also has state inspectors examining the books of every parochial school and the majority of parishes in both states. This poking of governmental noses into the inner workings of large numbers of churches is a perfect example of "excessive entanglement" for the Supreme Court.

It is easy to sympathize with the dissenting minority who complain that states who want to provide supplements to private school teachers are thus caught in a double bind that is impossible to satisfy. If the states fail to provide for reports, their statutes may well be found unconstitutional by providing support for religion and failing the second step. The requirement of reports throws the states into conflict with step three.

A somewhat clearer case for violation of the Establishment Clause was found in Ab*ington Township School District v Schempp*, 374 US 203 (1963). In this precursor to *Lemon* the issue was whether Pennsylvania could require that its public schools begin the day with reading of ten verses from the Holy Scriptures, followed by class recitation of the Lord's Prayer. Using a truncated version of what would later be the *Lemon* test (only steps 1 and 2 were mentioned and applied in *Abington Township*) the Supreme Court found that there was no non-religious purpose in forced exposure to the Sacred Books of Judaism and Christianity and forced recitation of Christianity's most basic prayer. Furthermore, limitation of exposure to the Bible and the Lord's Prayer clearly favored the two named religions in the first instance and Christianity in the second. Thus *Abington Township* banned prayer in the classroom which was organized and led by school officials.

# THE FREE EXERCISE CLAUSE

The First Amendment goes on to further forbid, with respect to religion, any government action "prohibiting the free exercise thereof." We refer to this clause as the **"Free Exercise Clause."** The leading case applying the Free Exercise Clause is *Braunfeld v Brown* , 366 US 599 (1961). There Braunfeld was an Orthodox Jew whose faith required him to do no work whatsoever on the Jewish Sabbath (from sundown Friday until sundown Saturday) and accordingly, he closed his retail furniture shop to comply with dictates of his religion.

Pennsylvania required that most retail stores statewide close on Sunday as a day set aside for rest and recreation. Braunfeld lost business, apparently a significant amount of business according to the report of the opinion, as a result of his Saturday closing and could not make up the lost profits. He asserts that a refusal on the part of Pennsylvania to allow him to open on Sunday amounted to a penalty imposed on him because of his Orthodox Jewish Faith. After all, the requirement of a day of rest for employees was satisfied by his *Saturday* closing.

The Supreme Court took the opportunity to explain what was prohibited by the Free Exercise Clause and the test to use to determine if it had been violated. Citing extensive case law going back to the previous century, the Supreme Court stated that the Free Exercise Clause prevented a state from making it illegal to have a religious belief or opinion, to force anyone to accept a religion, or to say or believe anything that was in conflict with his religious beliefs.

Of much greater difficulty are cases where *conduct* rather than belief is concerned. When a government makes it criminal for someone to do something which is required by his religion, or requires someone to do something on pain of prosecution which his religion tells him he must not do, a reviewing court must perform a balancing test. The court must determine that the interests of society in regulating this particular type of conduct are so important as to greatly outweigh the interests of the individual in practicing his religion. Thus, the interests of society in preventing death from other than natural or accidental causes would outweigh the religious freedoms of individuals who practiced human sacrifice.

This was not the case with Braunfeld. He was not faced with " . . . the choice to the individual of either abandoning his religious principle or facing criminal prosecution." (366 US at 605). Braunfeld was not faced with the choice of giving up his God or going to jail which is the situation which must occur for a potential violation of the Free Exercise Clause to exist. He was faced with a choice of giving up his profit or giving up his God. As the Supreme Court noted, many people give up money to participate in what they feel is a religious way of living. (The Biblical injunction to tithe comes to mind.) If such a choice results from state action (where that action applies to everybody and is not targeted to hurt a particular religion) then the Supreme Court in *Braunfeld* found that the question of a violation of the Free Exercise Clause did not arise.

The application of the balancing test to weigh the relative importance of society's interest on the one hand, and the individual's belief on the other in order to determine if there was a "compelling government interest" in regulating the particular type of conduct, was eliminated by the Supreme Court in the case of *Employment Division of Oregon v Smith,*494 US 872 (1990).

In that case, Smith had been fired from his job because he had violated the Oregon statute which prohibited taking peyote. Smith was a member of the Native American Church, an organization of long standing with sincere beliefs (and thus a religion as defined by cases under the Free Exercise Clause). As part of his religious services, Smith consumed peyote. This sacrament in the Native American Church is a difficult and time consuming ceremony involving fasting and meditation, not lightly entered into. Smith was subsequently fired from his job. As rightfully discharged from his job for violating the Oregon narcotics statute, Smith was also denied unemployment compensation which is where the Oregon agency came into the case.

Smith urges that his being denied unemployment benefits after discharge for religious reasons was just like a number of prior cases wherein the Supreme Court had found that such a denial was a violation of the Establishment Clause.

The Supreme Court disagreed and eliminated any balancing test whatever in deciding Free Exercise cases if the state action is a law that affects everyone (a "law of general application"). To allow anyone to state that his religion exempts him from a statute that applied to everyone would, in the opinion of the Supreme Court, risk anarchy and the breakdown of society in a nation with as many religions as we have. Further, those cases which have been cited in the past as standing for the successful application of the Free Exercise Clause were really some other constitutional right operating along with the Free Exercise Clause; never the Free Exercise Clause alone.

The effect of this decision, the elimination of the Free Exercise Clause in the case of most statutes, was reversed by the Religious Freedom Restoration Act of 1993 (42 USCA Section 2000bb et *seq.*)

# FREEDOM OF THOUGHT

The right to believe as you wish, referred to in some of the Free Exercise cases, was given much fuller consideration in the freedom of expression cases. The idea that there is a freedom of thought which underlies the express freedoms of speech and of the press was explicitly recognized in the case of *Stanley v Georgia,* 394 US 557 (1969). That case focused on freedom of thought because the expressions of freedom of the press involved were not protected by the First Amendment. Stanley was suspected of conducting illegal bookmaking activities and his house was raided pursuant to a properly issued search warrant. The police did not find anything that would support a conviction for wagering, but they did discover certain films which, when viewed on a handy projector in the house, were deemed obscene. This assessment was confirmed at Stanley's trial. He was convicted of possession of obscene materials.

Stanley asserted on appeal that his mere private possession, even of admittedly obscene materials, was protected by the First Amendment. Stanley argued that the anti-obscenity cases which upheld criminal prosecution in obscenity cases were only concerned with distribution and sale of such material.

The Supreme Court agreed that, even though unprotected by First Amendment rights of free speech and free press, the material deemed obscene in Stanley's private possession was protected because of an underlying freedom of ideas:

> It is now well established that the Constitution protects the right to receive information and ideas. . . . This right to receive information and ideas, regardless of their social worth, . . . is fundamental to our free society. (394 US at 564)

The Supreme Court was particularly concerned with the intrusion by the state into a person's private dwelling to interfere with his private thoughts:

> If the First Amendment means anything, it means that a State has no business telling a man, sitting alone in his own house, what books he may read or what films he may watch. Our whole constitutional heritage rebels at the thought of giving government the power to control men's minds. (394 US at 565)

From this "whole constitutional heritage", the freedom of thought necessarily extends to protect thoughts and beliefs which are not of the mainstream. "[The Constitution's] guarantee is not confined to the expression of ideas that are conventional or shared by a majority." (394 US at 566).

# FREEDOM OF SPEECH

The concept of protecting the circulation of ideas which are unpopular was given further explanation in *Cohen v California*, 403 US 15 (1971). In that case Cohen was charged with disorderly conduct. The "conduct" was defined as Cohen wearing a jacket which explicitly cursed the draft (it was 1968) while walking through the hallways of Los Angeles County Courthouse. Cohen did not make either a sound or a disturbance, but merely wore his jacket with its strongly-worded message until his arrest.

While generally disgusted with what was viewed as juvenile behavior on the part of Cohen, the Supreme Court did find that the action was protected as expressive speech. Indeed this was speech of a particularly protected kind—political speech, or speech concerned with political issues of the day. Clearly the draft and the fate of those drafted for the war in Southeast Asia was of great public interest in 1968. Interest which was of an even higher level among young men of draft age such as Mr. Cohen (here we may wish to paraphrase Ben Franklin that there is nothing which sharpens one's wits so wonderfully as the prospect of one's imminent demise). The majority opinion put the case for freedom of expression clearly:

> . . . The Constitutional right of free expression is powerful medicine in a society as diverse and populous as ours. It is designed and intended to remove governmental restraints from the arena of public discussion, putting the decision as to what views shall be voiced largely into the hands of each of us, in the hope that use of such freedom will ultimately produce a more capable citizenry and more perfect polity and in the belief that no other approach would comport with the premise of individual dignity and choice upon which our political system rests. (403 US at 24)

To those who would censor words or expressions because of their inherent vulgarity and bad taste, together with a concern that they might be inspiring people to behave in an inappropriate manner, the Supreme Court noted that official intervention by the government in the name of good taste or good order ran a terrible risk:

> Finally, and in the same vein, we cannot indulge the facile assumption that one can forbid particular words without also running a substantial risk of suppressing ideas in the process. Indeed, governments might soon seize upon the censor ship of particular words as a convenient guise for banning the expression of unpopular views. (403 US at 26)

## CLEAR AND PRESENT DANGER

The question of at what point speech may be restricted because of the danger the very act of speaking created was dealt with in the case of *Brandenburg v Ohio*, 395 US 444 (1969). Brandenburg was a leader of the Ku Klux Klan who was filmed at a meeting of the Klan in Ohio. Surrounded by hooded figures who periodically uttered phrases which could not be made out while burning a cross, Brandenburg made a speech which included the following,"We're not a revengeant organization, but if our President, our Congress, our Supreme Court, continues to suppress the white, Caucasian race, it's possible that there might have to be some revengeance taken." [this is an accurate quote]. Brandenburg was subsequently convicted of violating the Ohio Criminal Syndicalism Statute which made it a crime to advocate violence as a means of achieving political change. The Supreme Court was concerned that Brandenburg's words, assuming that they did advocate violence as a political strategy, were merely words. His somewhat sullen audience merely stood around and did nothing in furtherance of Brandenburg's proposed actions:

> ... *[W]e are here confronted with a statute which, by its own words and as applied, purports to punish mere advocacy and to forbid, on pain of criminal punishment, assembly with others merely to advocate the described type of action. (395 US at 449)*

The Supreme Court determined that mere words, without something more, without incitement of a mob to violent action at the time and place of the utterance, are not sufficient to create criminal liability. The Supreme Court refined the old "clear and present danger" doctrine that had been around for fifty years (given to us with Justice Holmes's image of "Fire!" in a crowded theater) to clearly mean danger created right here and right now by the simple act of speaking, or "imminent danger":

> ... *the constitutional guarantees of free speech and free press do not permit a State to forbid or proscribe advocacy of the use of force, except where such advocacy is directed to inciting or producing imminent lawless action and is likely to produce such action. (395 US at 447)*

## LIBEL AND SLANDER

Aside from the potential danger to public order which expression may pose under certain circumstances, there is also the harm which false and injurious statements cause to those who have been defamed (libelled or slandered) by a false statement. Defamation recognizes that not only may falsehoods cause real, if emotional, injury to the psyche of the person defamed. (Contrary to the child's nursery rhyme, although sticks and stones may break your bones, words can indeed hurt you by giving emotional distress and years of therapy.) In addition, there may well be economic repercussions in the business world as a result of the spread of falsehoods.

It is because of the possibility of both economic injury and emotional pain and suffering that the ancient English common law recognized the right to sue for compensation in cases of defamation almost seven hundred years ago. *Miller's Case*, in the early 1300's, allowed recovery for the following false and defamatory statement, "Dame Miller is a whore and hath the pox." The difficulty that we find ourselves in in this country is a tension between the principle of free expression on the one hand and the need to protect individuals from harm resulting from false and malicious statements on the other. A line of cases dealing with this tension was summed up in *Gertz v Robert welch, Inc.*, 418 US 323 (1974).

Gertz, who had acted as the lawyer for a family in a wrongful death action against a Chicago police officer and had not courted publicity, who was not a public official nor a figure in general public debate in any way, although active in local professional organizations, was accused in an article published by the defendant of being a "Leninist" and a member of a number of various Communist front groups (which in fact Gertz was not). The article was written by a free lance author that the defendant had used before with good response from readers.

The Supreme Court noted that defamation is an area of the law which states have a stake in. "The legitimate state interest underlying the law of libel is the compensation of individuals for the harm inflicted on them by defamatory falsehood" (418 US at 341). The Supreme Court noted that outright falsehoods had no place in the free flow of ideas that justifies free expression:

> . . . [T]here is no constitutional value in false statements of fact. Neither the intentional lie not the careless error materially advances society's interest in 'uninhibited, robust and wide open' debate on public issues. (418 US at 340)

Since there is no benefit to be gained from false statements, and since there may manifestly be harm that results from lies, intentional or unintentional, Why should false statements be given any First Amendment protection at all? Why shouldn't there be absolutely certain penalties imposed for statements which have no benefits and significant detriments, just as kiddie porn is punished wherever it is found? The answer lies in the **"chilling effect"** such action would have on any forum of debate if people were to be made absolutely liable for the truth of their statements in possible suits for damages if their statements prove untrue ("Chilling effect" is the legal expression of the old adage, "Once bitten, twice shy"):

> Although the erroneous statement of fact is not worthy of constitutional protection, it is nevertheless inevitable in free debate . . . .punishment of error runs the risk of inducing a cautious and restrictive exercise of the constitutionally guaranteed freedoms of speech and press. Our decisions recognize that a rule of strict liability that compels a publisher or broadcaster to guarantee the accuracy of his factual assertions may lead to intolerable self-censorship. Allowing the media to avoid liability only by proving the truth of all injurious statements does not accord adequate protection to First Amendment liberties. (418 US at 340)

The tension between the social necessities for open debate on the one hand and for protection of the individual from negligent or intentional harm on the other led the Supreme Court to create, over a series of cases prior to *Gertz*, the **public figure doctrine**. Statements, even false statements, about a public figure were protected except in the most extreme cases of misstatement:

> *Those who, by reason of the notoriety of their achievements or the vigor and success with which they seek the public's attention, are properly classed as public figures and those who hold governmental office may recover for injury to reputation only on clear and convincing proof that the defamatory falsehood was made with knowledge of its falsity or with reckless disregard for the truth [this is the New York Times test sometimes called 'actual malice'] (418 US at 342)*

Aside from the public policy of encouraging debate especially about policy issues of the day, the ability of public figures to defend themselves using the same means with which they were attacked is also considered:

> *Public officials and public figures usually enjoy significantly greater access to the channels of effective communication and hence have a more realistic opportunity to counteract false statements than private individuals normally enjoy. Private individuals are therefore more vulnerable to injury, and the state interest in protecting them is correspondingly greater. (418 US at 344)*

Finding that Gertz is a private individual within the meaning of the distinction, the Supreme Court recognizes that the interest of each state in protecting its citizens should allow each state to determine what the standard for liability will be for private figures, so long as there is no "strict liability." A publisher or broadcaster may not be held liable if it is not at fault in the publication of the falsehood, a position which

> *. . . recognizes the strength of the legitimate state interest in compensating private individuals for wrongful injury to reputation , yet shields the press from the rigors of strict liability for defamation. At least this conclusion obtains where, as here, the substance of the defamatory statement 'makes substantial danger to reputation apparent.' This phrase places in perspective the conclusion we announce today. Our inquiry would involve considerations somewhat different from those discussed above if a State purported to condition civil liability on a factual misstatement whose content did not warn a reasonably prudent editor or broadcaster of its defamatory potential. (418 US at 348)*

# FREEDOM OF THE PRESS

The question of whether or not a state could impose a more effective means of defense for an individual who felt wronged by a news story was considered in *Miami Herald Publishing Co. v Tornillo*, 418 US 241 (1974), which was decided shortly before *Gertz*.

There the state of Florida had a "right of reply" statute which purported to force any newspaper to carry the answer of a candidate for public office who felt he had been wronged by that news story. The Florida statute not only required that the newspaper print the candidate's reply, but that the reply be given the same prominence on the same page as the offending article. The Herald published editorials critical of Tornillo's candidacy for the Florida legislature and Tornillo sought to exercise his statutory right of reply which was backed up by the fact that failure to publish such a reply was a criminal misdemeanor.

The Herald appealed asserting that the right of reply statute was a violation of the guarantee of the freedom of the press. The Florida Supreme Court held that the right of reply statute increased the free flow of ideas and enhanced public debate by mandating that opposing views be published.

The Tornillo position was essentially that things had substantially changed since the early days of the republic when virtually anyone could start a newspaper to inject his own views into the public debate. The late Twentieth Century had seen a series of mergers and takeovers in the news media on both a national and a local scale. The result was that a great concentration of ownership had placed control of the news organs in a few hands, and in effect limited debate to the few voices who owned the media conglomerates. "The First Amendment interest of the public in being informed is said to be in peril because the 'marketplace of ideas' is today a monopoly controlled by the owners of the market" (418 US at 251).

Nevertheless, allowing a government to dictate what a newspaper *must* print was unconstitutional. "The clear implication has been that any such a compulsion to publish that which 'reason' tells them should not be published is unconstitutional" (418 US at 256).

The immediate cause of the finding is much the same as the public figure doctrine discussed in *Gertz*. The requirement acts as a penalty because the newspaper would be forced (given the economic realities of newspaper publication) to give up the publication of some other item to make room for the candidate's reply. The possibility of imposition of a penalty would cause a "chilling effect" on the newspaper's participation in public debate:

*Faced with the penalties that would accrue to any newspaper that published news or commentary arguably within the reach of the right-of-access statute, editors might well conclude that the safe course is to avoid controversy. Therefore, under the operation of the Florida statute, political and electoral coverage would be blunted or reduced. (418 US at 257)*

Aside from the failure of the Florida statute on its own terms, the Supreme Court sounded a warning against any government dictation to any newspaper in the presentation of the news:

*A newspaper is more than a passive vehicle or conduit for news, comment, and advertising. The choice of material to go into a newspaper, and the decisions made as to limitations on the size and content of the paper, and treatment of public issues and public officials —whether fair or unfair—constitute the exercise of editorial control and judgment. It has yet to be demonstrated how governmental regulation of this crucial process can be exercised consistent with First Amendment guarantees of a free press as they have evolved to this time. (418 US at 258)*

# ADVERTISING AND FREE EXPRESSION

A particular form of expression which may be regulated is advertising or, in law, "commercial speech." The case articulating the conditions under which advertisements may be regulated is *Posadas de Puerto Rico Assoc.v Puerto Rico Tourism Co.*, 478 US 328 (1986).

In that case the Tourism Company was the agency of the government of Puerto Rico which regulated all aspects of the tourist business in Puerto Rico, including the casino industry. (Recall that Puerto Rico is still officially part of the United States for the purposes of applying the Constitution to its citizens). Posadas operated a hotel and casino complex in Puerto Rico. The Tourism Company had legalized casino gambling almost forty years before the instant case, primarily to attract tourists and separate them from their money. The government of Puerto Rico, operating through its arm, the Tourism Company, did not want Puerto Rican citizens to be tempted by casinos. Officials believed that local participation in casino gambling would give rise to increased crime, prostitution and homelessness. To lessen the local participation, casino advertising was prohibited on Puerto Rico except for locations likely to reach tourists and unlikely to reach locals (such as the international terminal at the airport and major hotels).

Posadas sought to have the restriction on its advertising found unconstitutional as a denial of free speech and freedom of the press.

Advertising is, as a matter of constitutional law, not in the same class as the various kinds of expression we have considered so far. Our previous cases dealt with attempts to enter into debates on public policy and to attempt to influence public perceptions. In contrast to the prior cases' attempts to compete in the marketplace of ideas, advertising only wants to compete in the marketplace: "pure commercial speech . . . does no more than propose a transaction" (478 US at 340). Where our other free expression cases were motivated by idealism, however misplaced, advertising is motivated by the desire for commercial gain. Not being aimed at the free flowing exchange of ideas for their own sake, advertising is not given the same degree of protection as other forms of expression and may be regulated by the government in a broader range of situations:

> . . . commercial speech receives a limited form of First Amendment protection so long as it concerns a lawful activity and is not misleading or fraudulent. Once it is determined that the First Amendment applies to the particular kind of commercial speech at issue, then the speech may be restricted only if [1] {numerals added} the government's interest in doing so is substantial, [2] the restrictions directly advance the government's asserted interest, and [3] the restrictions are no more extensive than necessary to serve that interest. (478 US at 340)

Thus, commercials must pass a couple of hurdles before they can even pretend to have the slightest bit of protection from government regulation, up to and including an outright ban. The advertisements must be for a legal product and they must be truthful. (The reality of the advertising world is that there is a fair amount of latitude given in the degree of truthfulness permitted, a fact satirized in the Joe Isuzu commercials of a few years back starring David Leisure). Assuming that the commercials meet the first two tests, any government regulation can then be imposed only if the three criteria are satisfied.

The application of the three steps in validating the restrictions imposed by Tourism Company in *Posadas* can serve to illustrate the process. Clearly the casino industry was legal and presumably the advertisements were within the bounds accepted for truthfulness.

Having passed its first two thresholds, Posadas shifted the burden to the Tourism Company to show that its regulations are permitted under the limited constitutional protection enjoyed by Posadas' advertising. As to the question of a substantial government interest being involved, the Supreme Court noted that the evils that the Puerto Rican government believes accompany any local partici-pation in casino gambling are serious problems and that any government has a proper interest in attempting to prevent them from befalling its citizens.

As to a reasonable connection between the goals of the government and the means sought to achieve them, the Supreme Court noted that, after substantial inquiry, the Puerto Rican government generally and the Tourism Company in particular concluded that the restriction of local casino advertising was an effective way to limit local participation in casino gambling.

Finally, the fact that advertising was not banned altogether but only in those places likely to reach only local citizens, indicated that the restriction did not go farther than it had to in order to achieve the aim. Furthermore, the Supreme Court noted that the status of casino gambling as an underlying subject of advertising could be banned entirely in its own right. Aside from the fact that this would immediately raise the insurmountable hurdle of illegality before reaching the three step test:

> *It would just as surely be a strange constitutional doctrine which would concede to the legislature the authority to totally ban a product or activity, but deny the legislature the authority to forbid the stimulation of demand for the product or activity through advertising . . . (478 US at 346)*

# PRIOR RESTRAINT

A final look at the purposes behind freedom of thought and of expression can be seen in the decision in the Pentagon Papers case, more formally known as *New York Times Co. v United States*, 403 US 713 (1971). In that case a former Pentagon employee leaked documents about the origins of the United States' entry into the Vietnam War together with other documents detailing early U.S. participation in that war. Major national newspapers would publish a portion of the Pentagon Papers, only to be stopped by an injunction sought by the Executive Branch in the name of national security. Stopping a newspaper before it prints a story is called "prior restraint" and the Supreme Court lifted the injunction in a brief *per curiam* opinion with no named author. Then most of the justices wrote their own separate opinion concurring with or dissenting from the result.

Justice Black set forth his view of the role of a free press in our system of society and government:

> *In the First Amendment the Founding Fathers gave the free press the protection it must have to fulfill its essential role in our democracy. The press was to serve the governed, not the governors. The Government's*

*power to censor the press was abolished so that the press would remain forever free to censure the government. . . . Only a free and unrestrained press can effectively expose deception in government. And paramount among the responsibilities of a free press is the duty to prevent any part of the government from deceiving the people and sending them off to distant lands to die of foreign fevers and foreign shot and shell. (403 US at 717)*

The tests as to when prior restraint, an absolute foreclosure of debate, an end to the free flow of ideas and the competition in the marketplace of ideas, may be permitted show that only the most extreme and urgent danger can operate to limit the freedom of thought we started to consider with *Stanley v Georgia*. The two most workable tests are set forth by Justices Brennan and Stewart. They both use as a yardstick not just a state of war, but the most imminent danger in time of war. Justice Brennan writes:

*Our cases, it is true, have indicated that there is a single, extremely narrow class of cases in which the First Amendment's ban on prior judicial restraint may be overridden . . . .such cases may arise only when the nation 'is at war' . . . during which times '[n]o one would question that a government might prevent actual obstruction to its recruiting service or the publication of the sailing dates of transports or the number and location of troops. (403 US at 726)*

Justice Stewart sets forth a more philosophical test which places the only effective consideration to prematurely cut off debate and to limit the freedoms of belief, thought and expression

*[D]isclosure of any of them will surely result in direct, immediate, and irreparable damage to our nation or its people. (403 US at 730)*

Nothing less can constitutionally operate to limit thought.

## Chapter Exercises ❖      Rights

Name_____Section_____

1. Explain the operation of the *Lemon v Kurtzman* test in determining whether or not there has been a violation of the Establishment Clause.

2. Explain the concept of the "public figure doctrine" and how it contributes to the free flow of ideas and avoids a "chilling effect."

3. Explain the circumstances under which "prior restraint" may be imposed and why.

# CHAPTER NINE

# *Other Rights*

### Chapter Objectives

As a result of studying this chapter, the student should be able to perform the following activities:

1. Explain the circumstances under which the Second Amendment creates a right to bear arms.
2. Define the Exclusionary Rule and explain its operation and the reasoning behind its development.
3. Discuss the reasons listed in *Gideon v Wainwright* for the creation of a right to an attorney in criminal trials.
4. Explain the reasoning behind the *Miranda* Warning.
5. Explain how to figure out whether a sentence imposed on a criminal is cruel and unusual punishment.

## RIGHT TO BEAR ARMS

Although the civil rights associated with the First Amendment have given rise to a large number of cases arising under the Bill of Rights, most of the other amendments have also been considered. The Second Amendment, concerning the Right to Bear Arms, is one which has stirred a great deal of debate. The Second Amendment reads, in its entirety, "A well regulated Militia, being necessary to the security of a free State, the right of the people to keep and bear Arms, shall not be infringed."

The leading case in interpreting and applying the Second Amendment is *United States v Miller,* 307 US 174 (1939). Miller was a gangster who was caught and successfully prosecuted for violating the federal statute prohibiting possession of sawed-off shotguns. Miller argued that the National Firearms Act of 1934 was unconstitutional as an infringement on the right to keep whatever guns one felt necessary or desirable, urging that the language, " . . . the right of the people to keep and bear arms shall not be infringed" by its literal interpretation gave protection to the possession and carrying of guns.

The Supreme Court decided that the Second Amendment was a complete sentence and should be read as such. After noting that Article I, Section 8 of the Constitution gave to Congress as one of its enumerated powers, "To provide for organizing, arming, and disciplining, the Militia . . . " and that the Second Amendment must be interpreted as assuring the effectiveness of such militia forces. The Supreme Court defined the militia thusly:

> *The militia which the states were expected to maintain and train is set in contrast with Troops, which they were forbidden to keep without the consent of Congress. The sentiment of the time strongly disfavored standing armies; the common view was that adequate defense of the country could be secured through the Militia-civilians primarily, soldiers on occasion.( 307 US at 178–79)*

The court noted that, aside from their character as the military equivalent of a volunteer fire department, one thing that distinguished militia from regular troops is the fact that the militia provided their own arms from a list of approved weapons. (The Court opinion goes on at length about this, starting with Alfred the Great of England and moving forward through time.) Since the court cannot find any militia which approved sawed-off shotguns as part of its list of gear to be provided by its enrolled members, and since the right to bear arms is conditioned by membership in a "well regulated militia", the Second Amendment did not invalidate the National Firearms Act as it applied to Miller, who was not a member of a well-regulated militia and whose weapon was not approved for use by members of any such militia. Thus, the Second Amendment created a right to bear arms for those who were members of "a well-regulated Militia" rather than a general right to bear arms.

## DEFENDANTS' RIGHTS

The rights of defendants in criminal actions are conditioned by the so-called Big Three, which changed the face of state criminal trials in the 1960s. The first of the three cases to be decided was

*Mapp v Ohio*, 367 US 643 (1961), which applied the Fourth Amendment requirement for searches to states and enforced that requirement by applying the **Exclusionary Rule** to state criminal trials (improperly obtained evidence could not be introduced at trial—thereby removing the profit motive for police misconduct). The second case of the group to be decided was *Gideon v Wainwright*, 372 US 335 (1963), which required that states provide lawyers for defendants charged with felonies if they were too poor to hire one. The third case was *Miranda v Arizona*, 384 US 436 (1964), which extended the Exclusionary Rule to apply to improperly obtained statements where a suspect had not been adequately told of his rights as a criminal suspect (the list of warnings associated with television police dramas and the verb "to mirandize" come from this decision).

# MAPP v OHIO AND THE EXCLUSIONARY RULE

The facts in *Mapp* illustrate the problems associated with police misconduct generally. Miss Mapp was suspected of harboring a bomber in her home. The Cleveland police sought entry and were turned away at the door because they did not have a search warrant. After watching the house for some hours, the police forced their way in, waving about a piece of paper claimed to be a search warrant (since the paper does not reappear in any of the court cases, we can safely assume that it was not a warrant). Miss Mapp's attorney arrived during the search, but was denied access to his client. Miss Mapp herself was manhandled painfully and handcuffed. The extensive search did not turn up even a trace of the bomber originally sought. But in a trunk certain obscene materials were discovered, and it is for the possession of those obscene materials that Miss Mapp was convicted.

The Ohio authorities made no effort to justify their search as being pursuant to a properly issued warrant. They relied instead on the 1949 holding in *Wolf v Colorado* that even improperly obtained evidence could be admitted in state criminal trials as a matter of U.S. constitutional law.

The Supreme Court in *Mapp* quoted the 1886 case of *Boyd v United States* as setting forth the circumstances which would trigger a violation of the Fourth Amendment prohibition against illegal searches and seizures as well as the Fifth Amendment prohibition against forced self-incrimination:

> *[I]t is the invasion of [a person's] indefeasible right of personal security, personal liberty and private property\*\*\*Breaking into a house and opening boxes and drawers are circumstances of aggravation; but any*

*forcible and compulsory extortion of a man's testimony or of his private papers to be used as evidence to convict him of crime or to forfeit his goods is within the condemnation \*\*\*(367 US at 647, quoting 116 US at 635)*

As noted by the *Mapp* decision, the Supreme Court determined in *Weeks v United States*, 232 US 383 (1914), that evidence obtained in violation of the Fourth Amendment would be barred from use in criminal proceedings. The *Weeks* court reasoned that permitting the introduction of evidence improperly obtained would rob the Fourth Amendment of any meaning, rendering it nothing more than mere words on a page with no effective force in the real world.

The Supreme Court declined to extend the application of the Exclusionary Rule to state prosecutions in *Wolf*. The reasoning behind that decision was two-fold: 1) that so many states did not employ the exclusionary rule that its application to the states would cause great upheaval throughout the state criminal proceedings; and 2) the remedies that already existed to penalize the police for misconduct were sufficient to prevent any further wrongdoing on the part of the police.

The Supreme Court in *Mapp* observed that the factual considerations in *Wolf* no longer applied. More than half the states had adopted their own version of the exclusionary rule in the interim and the remedies for police misconduct were deemed to be "worthless and futile" in the *Mapp* decision. Since the reasons for the holding in *Wolf* had disappeared, the Supreme Court applied the Fourth Amendment to state proceedings, using the same means of enforcement (the exclusion of improperly obtained evidence at trial) as was applied to federal criminal proceedings.

Aside from the *Weeks* justification that failure to enforce the Fourth Amendment would render it meaningless, the Supreme Court also noted that the requirements of the Exclusionary Rule would not operate to hinder law enforcement, noting that the FBI performs its functions most effectively without chafing under federal restrictions. Aside from the practicalities of evidence gathering in law enforcement, the Supreme Court raised an important issue by quoting the dissent of Justice Brandeis in *Olmstead v United States*, 277 US 438 (1928):

*Our government is the potent, the omnipresent teacher. For good or ill, it teaches the whole people by its example\*\*\*If the government becomes a lawbreaker, it breeds contempt for the law; it invites every man to become a law unto himself; it invites anarchy (367 US at 659)*

# GIDEON v WAINWRIGHT AND THE RIGHT TO AN ATTORNEY

The philosophy behind *Mapp*, with its questions of"Who will guard the guardians?" and "What will happen if we all do as they do rather than as they say?" is replaced by straightforward consideration of nuts and bolts realities in *Gideon v Wainwright*, 372 US 335 (1963). Clarence Gideon, a career petty criminal (since he was frequently motivated by alcohol, a largely unsuccessful career as a petty criminal) was arrested for the crime of breaking and entering a poolroom with an intent to commit a misdemeanor, an overall offense classified as a felony. At trial Gideon asked that a lawyer be appointed to represent him, since he had no money (remember Gideon was an *unsuccessful* career petty criminal), and the Sixth Amendment guaranteed him the right to an attorney in criminal cases. The trial judge could not appoint one as Florida law provided that attorneys would be provided for indigent defendants only in capital cases. Convicted, Gideon was sentenced to five years and appealed.

The issue would seem to have been determined by the precedent of *Betts v Brady*, 316 US 455 (1942), which held that there was no obligation on the states to provide attorneys for the poor criminal defendant on largely similar facts. Despite the *Betts* precedent, the Supreme Court revisited the issue for a second look in *Gideon*. The Supreme Court in *Gideon* based its decision largely on two concepts:

1. the technical aspects of a criminal trial are beyond the experience of laymen and thus the procedural safeguards to protect rights cannot operate if the defendant does not know how to invoke them; and

2. the adversary system ceases to function if both sides are not more or less equal in the contest before the finder of fact (it was the failure of the contest by prearrangement that gave rise to the case or controversy rule on somewhat similar grounds).

With respect to the first basis for reversing *Betts* and requiring that attorneys be furnished for criminal defendant who were unable to pay for them, the Supreme Court noted that:

*Even the intelligent and educated layman has small and sometimes no skill in the science of law. If charged with crime, he is incapable, generally, of determining for himself whether the indictment is good or bad. He is unfamiliar with the rules of evidence . . . .He lacks both the skill and knowledge to prepare his defense, even though he have a perfect one. (372 US at 345)*

This lack of knowledge of the "magic language" and "mystic spells" of the law could not only have the practical effect of losing the criminal trial for a lay defendant, it could also work to deprive the defendant of his constitutional rights from lack of knowledge either of their existence or of the mechanism of enforcing them. For example, how could the constitutional right against improper searches and seizures given in the Fourth Amendment in *Mapp* above be enforced if the defendant didn't know that *Mapp* operated to keep improperly obtained evidence out of the criminal trial:

*From the very beginning, our state and national constitutions and laws have laid great emphasis on procedural and substantive safeguards designed to assure fair trials before impartial tribunals in which every defendant stands equal before the law. This noble ideal cannot be realized if the poor man charged with crime has to face his accusers without a lawyer to assist him. (372 US at 344)*

Aside from the defendant's need to effectively and vigorously protect his rights through assistance of an attorney, the operation of the judicial system, based upon the Anglo-Saxon adversary process, assumes that both sides will have adequate skill to efficiently present the strongest case for its side in a trial and to point out the weaknesses in the case presented by the other side. Failure of either side to perform these functions in at least an adequate manner frustrates the entire process:

*[I]n our adversary system of criminal justice, any person haled into court, who is too poor to hire a lawyer, cannot be assured a fair trial unless counsel is provided for him. This seems to be an obvious truth . . . .That government hires lawyers to prosecute and defendants who have the money hire lawyers to defend are the strongest indications of the widespread belief that lawyers in criminal courts are necessities, not luxuries. (372 US at 344)*

# MIRANDA v ARIZONA AND
# THE MIRANDA WARNING

The concepts that a person should only yield evidence against himself after procedural safeguards had ensured that all of a suspect's rights had been protected and that any information given by a suspect should be given voluntarily (forced revelations being suspect as unreliable for a variety of reasons) were extended in *Miranda v Arizona*, 384 US 436 (1964). In that case Ernesto Miranda was arrested for a variety of offenses, interrogated by police using approved techniques designed to "turn the suspect's brain into swiss cheese". The goal of the interrogation was to bring about a dependence by the suspect on his questioner and a desire on the part of the suspect to gratify the questioner. In effect this substitutes the will of the questioner for that of the suspect. The officers emerged from interrogating Miranda after a period of a few hours with a signed confession to kidnapping and rape and reports of oral confessions to that offense and an unrelated robbery that he was also convicted of in a separate trial.

The Supreme Court held that the confession should not have been permitted into evidence at trial because Miranda was not informed of the consequences of his statements, his rights to keep silent and to an attorney. The Supreme Court was particularly concerned in the opinion with certain consequences of the practice of "custodial interrogation" or "holding for investigation." These are consequences in which the innocent were locked up while the search for the guilty continued, often on little evidence.

In addition to the bad results of the practice of interrogating suspects without informing them of their rights, the Supreme Court was impressed with the excellent results achieved by organizations which did require full information of suspects. The FBI, which the Supreme Court during the Warren Court era felt was the finest law enforcement organization around, was cited as an example of law enforcement that did their job while using the warnings. The Supreme Court also noted with approval criminal investigations and prosecutions under the Uniform Code of Military Justice in the armed forces, as well as investigations and prosecutions in British Commonwealth countries such as India and in Scotland.

Despite the fact that the standard *Miranda* warnings have become a staple of police dramas as a way of indicating that a culprit has finally been apprehended, the *Miranda* decision specifically excludes any particular magic formula of words to be employed so as to ward off the Exclusionary Rule. The overall standard adopted to judge the warning given for effectiveness gives insight into the goals of the Supreme Court in its *Miranda* holding:

> ... the Constitution does not require any specific code of procedures for protecting the privilege against self-incrimination during custodial interrogation. Congress and the States are free to develop their own safeguards for the privilege, so long as they are fully as effective as

*those described above in informing accused persons of their right of silence and in affording a continuous opportunity to exercise it. (384 US at 490)*

Earlier in the text of the *Miranda* opinion (in contrast to the other lengthy examples in the footnotes from other examples of acceptable pre-interrogation warnings) the Supreme Court had paraphrased the wording of the procedure of the FBI, language which served as the ancestor of the precise warning that we have seen so often on television:

*Over the years the Federal Bureau of Investigation has compiled an exemplary record of effective law enforcement while advising any suspect or arrested person, at the outset of an interview, that he is not required to make a statement, that any statement may be used against him in court, that the individual may obtain the services of an attorney of his own choice and, more recently, that he has the right to free counsel if he is unable to pay.(384 US at 483)*

# CRUEL AND UNUSUAL PUNISHMENT

Another aspect of defendants' rights (more properly rights of people who have moved beyond defendant status into that of prisoner because they have been convicted) is the meaning of the Eighth Amendment prohibition against cruel and unusual punishment. The leading case in the area of determining whether a penalty constitutes cruel and unusual punishment within the meaning of the Amendment is *Solem v Helm,* 463 US 277 (1983). In that case Helm was convicted of passing a bad check for $100. Ordinarily the maximum penalty for this action would have been a maximum fine of $5000 and a maximum jail sentence of five years. However, Helm was convicted under the South Dakota recidivist or repeat offender statute. He had previously been convicted of six felony offenses such as DUI and obtaining money under false pretenses. (Helm's offenses all seemed to be a result of a serious problem that he had with alcohol, in his own words in the instant case,"I knew I'd done something I didn't know exactly what . . . .I was drinking and I didn't remember . . . " (463 US at 281)

Helm was sentenced to life without possibility of parole, which in South Dakota meant what it said. The only way Helm could get out of prison was a pardon by the governor. Since South Dakota did not have the death penalty at the time, "Helm's sentence is the most severe punishment that the State could have imposed on any criminal for any crime" (463 US at 297) including multiple first degree murder. The Supreme Court noted that even a heroin dealer convicted for a fourth time would not have been punished as severely, since the life sentence for a heroin dealer would carry the possibility of parole.

The Supreme Court seized on this as an opportunity to define the standards for the application of the Eighth Amendment, summarizing previous decisions interpreting the Amendment and setting out the criteria to be employed in determining whether a punishment was excessive:

> *In sum, a court's proportionality analysis under the Eighth Amendment should be guided by objective criteria, including (i) the gravity of the offense and the harshness of the penalty; (ii) the sentences imposed on other criminals in the same jurisdictions; and (iii) the sentences imposed for the commission of the same crime in other jurisdictions. (463 US at 292)*

The Court then applied its general criteria to Helm. In determining the gravity of the offense, the Court indicated that both considerations of harm done to the victim and/or society should be made as well as whether or not the offender was acting intentionally or negligently. In Helm's case, the Court reiterated that the crime was "one of the most passive felonies a person could commit," (463 US at 296) and that it resulted from Helm's drunkenness rather than any evil intent.

The Court contrasted that unintentional passivity with the severity of the sentence. In comparing sentences imposed by the same jurisdiction for other crimes, the Supreme Court noted that other serious crimes (such as the fourth conviction for sale of heroin noted above) carried lesser sentences, and that the mandatory nature of Helm's LWOPP sentence made it a more severe sentence than that of first time convictions for treason, manslaughter, first degree arson and kidnapping (where the imposition of a life sentence was discretionary with the sentencing judge). Finally the Supreme Court compared Helm's status as a repeat offender to sentences imposed by other states for that crime and found that only Nevada imposed the same sentence. In finding Helm's sentence to be in violation of the Eighth Amendment, the Supreme Court summed up its findings and conclusions:

> *The Constitution requires us to examine Helm's sentence to determine if it is proportionate to his crime. Applying objective criteria, we find that Helm has received the penultimate sentence for relatively minor criminal conduct. He has been treated more harshly than other criminals in the State who have committed more serious crimes. He has been treated more harshly than he would have been in any other jurisdiction, with the possible exception of a single State. We conclude that his sentence is significantly disproportionate to his crime and is therefore prohibited by the Eighth Amendment. (463 US at 303)*

## Chapter Exercises ❖ Other Rights

Name_____Section_____

1. Explain the operation of *Miller v United States* on Second Amendment cases.

2. Explain the "Exclusionary Rule" and how it was applied in *Mapp v Ohio* and *Miranda v Arizona.*

3. Explain how to go about figuring out if a sentence imposed on a defendant violates the Eight Amendment.

# Index

**115**